DECLUTTERING

SUSTAINABLY

How to Declutter Your Home with Minimal

Impact to the Environment with a Goal to

Live a Simple and Fulfilling Life

By
Harriet Webb

CONTENTS

INTRODUCTION

W hile the world is in love with minimalistic trends, many of us struggle to adopt these trends. Maybe you don't shove your way to the front, commando-roll under the shutters, or wait several hours to ensure you grab the best product deals on a shopping day. But you may look forward to the end-of-season sales, right? After all, everyone enjoys receiving discounts. However, the extra stuff eventually makes its way to your house, taking you further away from living a minimalistic life.

The overflowing magazine rack, the dining room filled with hundreds of decoration pieces, the staircase holding several plants, and the side table holding a week's worth of mail indicates the idea of consumption, collection, and purchasing has done something wrong to your life and house. Hence, lead to a cluttered house. You might not realise it at the time of purchasing that too much stuff in your house can only drain and frustrate you. It will make it difficult to get simple things done properly. Living in a cluttered space may cause the feeling of suffocation in your own house or could cause severe stress to yourself.

The constant life challenges and paralysing emotional attachments might make seeing any problem with your cluttered space impossible. What one person calls clutter, others might refer to it as treasure and collections. So, therefore before I recommend that you start practising sustainable decluttering methods, the first thing you need to do is to understand the definition of clutter.

So, what is clutter? Well, it's a tricky one to define. For one person, clutter means not being able to find the surface of the table. For others, it means not being able to manage piles of papers accumulated on the coffee table. The basic definition is anything untidy and messy in your space or a mess that's got out of control or needs sorting out. If you want to be more precise, clutter covers or fills space with disordered or scattered things that reduce effectiveness or movement. Hence, if you have so many books in the corner of your room or your kitchen is filled with crockery that you might not have used in ages, you might be dealing with clutter.

So, if you are struggling with this issue, you might need to declutter the space. I understand that clutter control is difficult, especially when your sentiments and emotions are attached. Obviously, the things you have purchased or collected are important to you somehow. We all have memories and feelings attached to different things. However, when cabinets, drawers, and wardrobes start to overflow, it becomes important to see the problem developing in your space and start doing something to resolve it.

Don't worry! You are not alone in it. I, Harriet Webb, will help you walk through this problem and get you out of it successfully. Wondering how? I have written this book, "Decluttering Sustainably", to help you practice techniques to declutter your house without impacting the environment and hurting your feelings. Trust me, it is not as difficult as we think, and the results you get will change your life in a good way. It will improve your mental health, boost productivity, and make it easy to manage your house.

I grew up in a cluttered environment, and consumerism has always been part of my life. But in my late 20s, I realised I was on the wrong path and started focusing on living a more sustainable life. As a result, I made a major decision to declutter my house by practising sustainable methods. This not only changed the outlook of my property but also had positive effects on my mental health. Over time, I have realised that my house's new, clean, and organised look has improved my mood, sharpened my focus, and energised my body. So, if I can do it, you can do it too!

Since sustainable decluttering has improved my life, I want to empower others to do the same and reap the benefits we often ignore.

"Decluttering Sustainably" is a book that offers you various aspects of cluttering and decluttering so you understand the reason behind it. Each chapter of the book will take you closer to decluttering your house without having to go through the emotional turmoil of letting go of things you're attached to. Every chapter is written to help you unfold the benefits of decluttering your space and keeping it organised and clean. I have also emphasised sustainable options for decluttering to avoid causing negative environmental effects. The sustainable methods help you make less to no waste. Opting for such ways that cause a positive impact on the Earth, make you feel fulfilled, and save you from feeling stressed or overwhelmed.

The first chapter, "Why We Over-Consume", will highlight the reasons for the habit of collecting things. This will help you decode the reason why you tend to clutter. Keep in mind that overconsumption not only has negative effects on your house but also leads to harmful impacts on the environment. It can create a great amount of waste of water, energy, and resources.

You will also learn about the science behind shopping habits and why they bring you satisfaction. Most importantly, this chapter will discuss the primary culprit of your uncontrolled shopping habits. Besides that, I have also emphasised the fact that overconsumption can impact our planet. Lastly, you will get some tips to stop yourself from making impulse purchases and regain control of your spending habits.

Chapter two, "Why We Find It Hard To Part With Our Possessions", will answer the most common problem of most homeowners. You will learn why we attach sentimental value to some objects and why parting with them is hard. I have also discussed why it is important to let go of things when they are not in use. We know it's hard to let go of things like a memorable piece of jewellery that someone special has gifted you or clothes you purchased with your first salary. Therefore, I have discussed how you can easily part with items close to your heart. This book will list some tips to make the process easy for you.

"Tidy House, Tidy Mind" is the third chapter that details the benefits of organising and clearing the house. You will learn the physical and mental health benefits of decluttering. For instance, it will help you get better sleep and reduce stress. It will also explain how decluttering space will help improve your productivity. Yes, you heard it right. Read further to know how.

After that, chapter 4, "Where To Start", will discuss the best approach to decluttering. The chapter covers steps to declutter the house to help you manage things at your place. You will also get tips and tricks that help you choose what you can keep and what you need to eliminate. This chapter will set the base for how you dispose of, throw, or donate your stuff. You can also recycle things to get rid of the clutter from your property. At all times, special emphasis is laid on sustainability and protecting the environment.

Chapter 5, "Saying Motivated," will highlight how you can stay motivated throughout decluttering. The chapter will discuss how to manage your feelings during decluttering, make quick decisions, and stick by them when the going gets tough.

Chapter 6, "How To Dispose Of Unwanted Things Sustainably," will discuss some common things people collect that need decluttering. You will get suggestions on how to declutter particular items by practising sustainable methods and limiting your impact on the Earth. This book discusses how to dispose of various objects, such as clothing, toys, and electrical equipment.

Now that you have learned how to declutter your house, chapter 7 will discuss "How To Maintain A Clean And Clutter-Free Environment." This chapter will list tips you can practice daily to simplify your life. You will learn to develop a mindset to help you live in a spacious, clean, clutter-free house.

The 8th and last chapter, "Helping Others", will tell you how you can help others who have been dealing with the same problem. This chapter will provide tips for supporting others in their decluttering journey and to help make their lives easier. You will learn how to empower others whilst remaining sensitive to their situation.

So, if you are ready to change your life and offer your family a clean and beautiful space, this book is a true blessing. Once you have finished reading it, please share it with others to inspire and help your friends and family to leverage the benefits of decluttering. Not to forget, you're also taking care of your clutter sustainably, playing your part in protecting Mother Earth for generations to come.

So, let's dig in!

Harriet Webb

Chapter 1

WHY DO WE OVER-CONSUME?

P icture this scenario: It's your friend's birthday, and you're visiting the shops to get something for them. You're super excited to see so many options to choose from. You got just what you're looking for. But the latest collection is too good not to get something for yourself. You're trying hard not to spend on something you don't need but can't hold yourself back. Your emotions take over, and you end up splurging on things you don't actually need. You got a dress for yourself. But just as you're about to head out, you find the perfect pair of trainers that will look amazing with your dress. You start rethinking. You are thinking about whether you should get the shoes or not, and after a continuous back and forth, you finally get the shoes too. This leads to a hefty bill. And above all, you have more stuff that you now have to store at your place. You already had quite a few pieces and didn't need anything new, but you could not resist your shopping urge.

Soon afterwards, your feelings change. You start feeling guilty about your purchase. In fact, you started to feel anxious about the amount of money you paid for it. According to the experts, that's the emotional roller coaster of shopping. Every pound you spend has an emotional cost. It's not about you. Many people experience this, and it has scientific reasons.

Everything you feel before, during, and after shopping is due to hormones. Researchers have explored the connection between shopping and the hormone dopamine. Dopamine is linked with excitement; it offers a thrill while hunting for a product in shops. It keeps you motivated until you find the perfect thing you've been looking for.

At the same time, your body starts producing cortisol, associated with regretful feelings like shame and guilt, and in this case, buyer's remorse. With cortisol in your body and dopamine levels reducing with time, you start to feel anxious and regret purchasing things you did not even need. You start regretting your decisions. As a result, you might often end up not using the thing you bought out of guilt or anxiety. This leads to piling of things and cluttering up our properties. The sad reality is that we repeat the same patterns the next time we go shopping. And because we couldn't enjoy the feeling of getting a new thing, we again get on a hunt to find something new to purchase. As a result, we overconsume and fill our houses with unnecessary and unwanted things that we may only occasionally use.

It's important to remember the discussed phenomenon every time you desperately feel the urge to get something for yourself or scroll through online stores. This will not only keep clutter away from your house but also saves you money and time that you can invest in more promising things. Not to mention, it saves you from the frustration of decluttering your spaces every few months.

Does Overconsumption Impact Our Planet?

Before we get to the environmental effects of overconsumption on the planet, it is important to understand what it is. It simply means individuals are consuming more resources that the Earth can provide than they need. Overconsumption also causes problems in the natural renewal of resources due to the higher speed of consumption. Besides that, overconsumption impacts the Earth in multiple ways, such as being a cause of higher production of greenhouse gasses or producing waste while disposing or decluttering. To be precise, the resources mined, transported, or used are the major factors that affect the environment. Here are a few things you need to know about how producing items you purchase causes problems for the Earth. Let's begin reading!

Mining of Resources and Overconsumption

Most metals used to produce electronic devices you use daily are mined through unethical labour methods. Metal is everywhere: our cars, offices, homes, public buildings, public transport, etc. Keep in mind that 2.8 billion tonnes of metals were mined only in 2021. Mining for metal doesn't come without a price, as it produces air pollution, destroys the ecosystem, and chemicals and oils usually spill and contaminate the natural surroundings.

Deep sea mining is another modern practice to meet the demands of the products in the market. We might not stop companies from mining, but we certainly stop or reduce purchasing items that lead to this devastating practice.

Transportation of the Resources

Not only do you need to consider the extraction of the resources, but you need to also consider their transportation. T Consider the smartphone as an example. The materials needed to produce its different parts are sent to various factories, where they assemble parts. Once made, these parts are transported to the main mobile factory, which generates emissions. And when the smartphone is made, it is sent across the country to numerous storage facilities. Then the item is shipped to a house if it's bought online or goes to a shop for sale.

Throughout the journey of the production of smartphones, one thing is common: the emission of gasses and the use of energy. Unfortunately, most factories have not switched to renewable energy sources, making them the main cause of global warming.

The more you consume, the more logistic transportation occurs, and the more fossil fuels we burn. And when more fossil fuels are burned, more mining will be needed to get fossil fuels, and the hotter the Earth will get.

Overconsumption Effects are Not Immediately Obvious

It's important to understand that the environmental effects of overconsumption are not seen immediately. It takes years to impact the Earth. 20% of the world's population consumes 80% of the Earth's resources. Humans use and extract 50% more natural resources than three decades ago. People from developed countries are the most responsible for the human impact on the Earth. Yet, they are the people least impacted by the polluted environment.

It's important to stop overconsuming things to protect the planet and help people who will be most affected by the negative effects of overconsumption.

Overconsumption Leads to Waste

People who over-consume things will eventually throw or dispose of these items. This wastes resources and produces a great amount of waste that can impact the environment. The waste generated by humans is detrimental to our environment. We are generating too much waste and not opting for more sustainable disposal methods. Waste that can't be recycled or properly biodegraded is filling our landfills and oceans. So, even if your consumption habit doesn't cause clutter in your house, as you throw things away, it will still impact the Earth. And as it causes environmental issues, it will eventually impact you or your next generation's life.

Sustainable Consumption

You can replace your overconsumption habit with sustainable consumption. While you will still buy things, choosing sustainable options will greatly save the planet and help resolve plastic pollution and the climate crisis.

While it's true that sustainable products will need energy and resources to be produced and transported, they are better than alternative products. Since there are fewer sustained products in the market, you need to take some time to search for them.

Additionally, never believe an advertisement for sustainable products. You need to look for a few factors to ensure its sustainability. Here are the things you need to consider to decide whether the products are sustainable.

- It has natural and fewer ingredients.

- The product is biodegradable or made from recycled materials.
- It can be recycled in future.
- The product is transported sustainably.
- The production process of items has generated little to no waste.

Consumers have a big impact on how companies participate in sustainability and what goals they set. Demand drives sales; therefore, if consumers choose not to spend money with companies that are not doing enough to protect the Earth, they will lose profit. This is causing companies to consider ways to reduce their environmental impact.

Marketing and Targeted Advertising - Turning Wants into Needs Leading to Overconsumption

The "need" is something you require to live a life - it's a necessity. We all need shelter, food, clothes, and other basic things. A "want" is something you desire to have but can live without it. Marketing and targeted advertising can turn our wants into needs. They make us believe that the particular product they are selling is essential to living a happy and good life, and without it, you might miss out on something or struggle to do particular activities.

You might think it's obvious, and this phenomenon is a no-brainer. But try explaining that to a teenager who wants the latest Android product or a mum who wants to give their child the latest toys in the market to keep them happy. Well, you will obviously have a hard time explaining to them because they think they "need" it. This is the power of marketing and advertising. While advertisements may not seem harmful, they change our perspective and mindset, leading to a never-ending desire to purchase new things, fill our houses and create cluttered spaces.

Advertisers craft messages strategically to turn wants into perceived needs. Don't believe me? Well, think about all the things you have to do that you consider necessary, but years ago, it was described as luxuries. This includes a Smartphone, different types of crockery sets for a house of few people, wireless internet, convenience meals and fast foods, automatic toys like cars, branded clothes, and many others.

Marketing has successfully established the belief that the above products are something we can't live without through commercials, newspaper ads, product placements in movies, targeted advertisements on social media platforms, and other techniques. However, some can recall peaceful, joyful, and fulfilling lives without them. Today, we don't feel satisfied until we fill our kitchen cabinets, wardrobes, and other spaces and challenge ourselves to keep them organised and clean.

A successful marketing message transcends the target customer's perceptions of needs and wants. It creates an emotional appeal that unconsciously convinces the audience that the product they are promoting will make a great difference in their lives. It can give them status, make them happy, provide security, or satisfy a desire. We all know that a well-design advertisement promotes sales. These sales appeal to buyers by encouraging them to rationalise their wants that they might otherwise suppress and resist. The potential customer feels that they need to purchase the item now. If not, the discounted prices will be gone, and the price will increase afterwards. The terror of a price increase again forces people to buy several clothes, toys, shoes, and other things, and then they struggle to declutter their houses.

Keep in mind that marketing tactics are not impacting the spaces of your house but also causing detrimental effects on our planet. The more things you purchase under the influence of target marketing, the more energy, water, and resources factories will use and waste, affecting the environment. On top of that, when you decide to declutter your house, you may recycle a few things, donate some, and dispose of a few things. And you might not know, but improper disposal contributes to excess gas production into the atmosphere. In addition, the breakdown of waste produces gases like methane, a primary factor in global climate change. So, even if you over-consume only sustainable products, overconsumption will still cause problems for you. And if you simply buy whatever things you want and you declutter, you will be negatively impacting our planet. Hence, overconsumption in any way is not an ideal approach.

The Solution: Learn to Balance Needs and Wants

The distinction between necessities and wants is determined by your circumstances and age. A woman might feel that a particular type of furniture is a need rather than a want for their house. Mothers who want to provide the best for their children might believe that branded clothes and expensive shoes are their kids' needs. Feeling the desire to buy things by considering you need them causes clutter in your house and wastes your hard-earned money.

Balancing your needs and wants is crucial for your pocket, house, and environment. The simplest way to stop thinking of your wants as needs is to evaluate whether the product you want to choose is your need or want. You need to classify your wants and needs according to your monthly earnings and financial health. Next, consider whether the product you plan to purchase is something you can't live without. Is it something that can truly impact your life? Also, consider whether the product will cause clutter in your space. These questions will help you decide whether to purchase the items and prevent clutter, harmful effects on the earth, and waste of money.

Change Your Mindset and Behaviour to Prevent Decluttering

Before jumping into the decluttering process, you must embrace new mindsets. Let's suppose you successfully declutter your space. Every corner of your house has started to look clean, organised, and beautiful. But out of your habit, you continue to purchase new items, clothes, and furniture without removing anything from your home. Over time, unfortunately, all the effort and energy you put into decluttering will go in vain. To stop this from happening, you need to change your attitude, behaviour, and perspective towards shopping. Real progress in terms of organisation and decluttering requires rethinking what we value and changing our mindsets.

Trust me; this approach will truly help you improve your life. Since I have been practising decluttering techniques and educating myself about them for years, I believe the following tactics can help you ignore the yearning to shop and help in controlling your clutter. Once you master them, you can proceed to the next step: decluttering. Here are a few things that might help you overcome your habit of overconsumption:

1.   Digital Detox

A digital detox is a technique to reduce screen time temporarily to be more present in the physical world and, most importantly, to break addictive patterns. While digital detox is commonly used to help improve your mood, relationships, and sleep, it can also help minimise your desire to purchase things.

Let's face it most of the brands, products, or discounted offers that come across to you are through the digital world. Startups, small businesses, or bigger corporations create strategically targeted advertisements to interact with and encourage potential customers to buy their products. Since they are so good at what they do, when you see the ad, you immediately feel the urge to buy it, which can often lead to an unintended purchase.

Digital detox is an ideal way to become aware of your online habits and their risks. By avoiding social media sites, emails, and other things, you can save yourself from the irresistible urge to buy things all the time. The digital detox will also help you realise that you don't need to shop for everything you see online because you don't need them. It's a scam that you fall into every time. This was a life-changing discovery for me, and I'm sure it will be for many of you. So, when you return to the digital landscape, you will know that the ads you see are only designed to make you believe you need them.

Are you wondering what things to avoid during your detox period? You need to avoid social media platforms, emails, search engines, marketing messages, and brand websites for a specific period, such as a couple of days or a week. During this time, rethink your shopping habits and behaviours to prepare yourself to emerge back into the digital world.

Here are a few tips for practising to successfully do a digital detox:

•   Mute Notifications

Out of all the apps you have on your phone, how many are truly important? Social interactive apps are unessential, as nothing urgent will happen on these apps. So, mute notifications of every unnecessary app. The information you will receive when a notification comes on your screen is not worth your time, especially if it's an ad. When you turn off the notifications, you will feel less urge to check your phone and fall into the trap of any marketing. Not to mention, you can enjoy your life and feel gratitude for what you have during this period. Of course, you can't get away from technology completely. Therefore, you can set a specific time of the day to check your magazines, newsletters, private messages, and whatever you keep active.

•   Consume Digital Information Mindfully

You need to consume digital information mindfully, not passively. This means you should go to it when needed, not when marketers decide to interact with you. When you keep all the apps at hand and all the notifications active, you will be tempted to check them, leading to passive checking and scrolling. Don't let them get to you. In fact, you should be the one to go to them when you truly need something for yourself, your family, or your house, and when you evaluate, it will not add to the clutter.

•   Use Phone with Purpose

Never use the phone to kill time. Of course, there is nothing bad about being online or connected to the internet world. The problem arises when we start doing this involuntarily and uncontrollably. When bored, we typically open our phone lock and start scrolling for no reason. We see something online and instantly add it to the cart. Eventually, this becomes our habit, making life in our house difficult due to unorganised cabinets, stuffed room corners, and a stack of garbage on tables. If you don't want your house filled with unnecessary items, think twice about everything you reach to a phone. Think do you really need to check your phone? If not, look for alternate activities to keep yourself busy, such as hanging out with friends, walking, or cooking a delicious meal.

- Establish Boundaries

If you are not willing to leave your mobile for a couple of days, you can choose certain times during the day and night when you will not use your phone. That way, when you use your mobile, you may only check messages, make a couple of calls, or read a newsletter when you have the mobile. Furthermore, you can establish a physical boundary of using the phone in a specific place, such as in a store while running errands or living room while having coffee. While it's true that AI tools are so powerful that they will try to reach you in this limited time, you might avoid them because you do not have enough time to check out an advertisement.

2.   Ask Questions to Yourself

Another thing you can do to create a mindset is to ask yourself a series of questions before you decide to buy anything. The following are the questions you need to ask:

- Does this item have a purpose that can't be met with something I already own?
- Would it be a great idea to rent or borrow this item from somewhere else rather than purchasing it?
- Is there any place in my house to keep it when I purchase it, or would I need to throw out something else?
- Can it change my life in a good way or positively impact my family?

Asking these questions will help you determine whether you need the item. It gives you time to think, rather than just visiting the brand site and purchasing whatever you think you need. Also, give yourself 24 hours to get an answer to these questions. And if you still justify buying an item throughout the day, go ahead.

This technique works amazing for those without budget issues and who buy anything they find attractive. By only practising this tactic, you can reduce your desire to shop for yourself or your family or friends, leading to fewer stored items in your house.

3.   Fight "Just in Case" Impulses

This is a big problem for most people, especially those responsible for their families, who want to facilitate them as much as possible. It's so easy to buy pick up different things in different places that homeowners purchase because of thinking "just in case." You might not be sure whether you need it, but you worry or think you might need it in the future.

This type of shopping might give you the sense that you are on top of things, but you are actually creating more work for yourself. You need to think about where to keep it. Should you give it to someone? Can you return it? How do you store it without impacting the appeal of your space? People usually ignore these decisions, and the products they purchase end up cluttering their places. This shopping behaviour leads to dozens of purchases that clutter your house and can cause stress.

Try to avoid buying items just in case. Avoid impulse purchases or buying an item only because you fear you will need it in the future. Instead, specify a waiting period for most purchases, whether it's a physical store or online shop. Put the item in your virtual cart and wait 24 hours before buying. In the case of a physical store, go home and spend a day thinking about whether you actually need it before returning to buy.

4.   Understand Your Motivation

Most women homeowners have a couple of categories of items that they are inclined to overbuy. For some, it's food. For many people, it's books and clothing. For others, it can be children's toys. Take some time to consider why you feel compelled to purchase those items. Do you like how it feels to buy a new jumpsuit, toy, or book, do numerous pots and dishes make you feel you can easily cook, or do you worry about running out of food? Be mindful of what is motivating you to purchase those items. And if buying a thing is important, at the very least, remove or dispose of one item from your house from the same category to keep your house organised and clean. When you put a lot of effort and thought into purchasing a thing, you will likely avoid making wrong decisions.

5.   Keep in Mind that More Doesn't Mean Better

Everyone is pressured to keep up with those around them in today's modern society. When we see our neighbours and friends wearing designer clothes and the latest gadgets, we feel we must keep up with them. On top of that, advertisements on TV tell us to believe in their products and that we must buy them to stay happy. But "more doesn't mean better." Just because someone has a nicer car or the latest branded clothes doesn't mean they live a more peaceful and happier life than yours. Don't fall into the trap of believing that you need more things to feel fulfilled. In fact, you need to focus on quality over quantity. Buy items that are important and bring joy to your life, and leave the rest. Feeling happy about everything you already have is key to living a good life and avoiding clutter in your house.

Choose Alternate Methods to Gain Fulfilment and Joy

If you are deprived of joy and fulfilment in your life, there are several other ways to gain them other than shopping. As I have discussed, shopping can boost your dopamine levels for a specific period. The things I have discussed below will increase serotonin levels and reduce the production of cortisol for a long time, making you feel happy and less stressed at the same time. So, if you ever desperately want to scroll through an online store to get the excitement and joyful feeling, you should opt for below alternative methods.

Spend Time with Family and Friends

Social time is significantly valuable for increasing your happiness-even for introverts. Many researchers suggest that time spent with family and friends greatly affects your happiness. I love how Daniel Gilbert, a Harvard College Professor of Psychology at Harvard University, explains in research that you feel happy when you have family, you are happy when you have friends, and all the other things you believe that make you happy are just ways to expand your social circle.

Help others as Much as you can

Want to get a real boost of happiness? Start helping others around you. One of the most counterintuitive pieces of advice I got is to help people to stay happier. You should try to make life easier and more joyful for others.

Spending money on other people is "prosocial spending", which boosts happiness. Therefore, research indicates that helping others brings people more joy than acquiring items for themselves. And what about spending our precious time with other people? Does it make you happy? Yes, it does.

If giving your time and energy makes others happy, secure and improves their lives, you will feel accomplished and contented. You can observe the change in your mood, behaviours, and body language after helping others. In short, helping others can improve your own life. It helps you overcome the feeling of joy when your shop, which eventually helps you avoid clutter. At the same time, consuming sensibly will also help protect the environment.

Meditate

Meditation is an ideal way to improve your life. It provides you with attention span and clarity as well as keeps you calm. Besides that, it can also help you boost your happiness. Meditation calms you down and clears your mind. It's one of the most effective ways to live a happier life. Meditation boosts your levels of happy hormones, making you feel calmer and more satisfied.

With meditation, you can control your mind and body. You can reduce stress, manage thoughts, and learn to make the right decisions. When you meditate regularly, you don't feel the need to rely on other things to feel happy, such as shopping. In fact, meditation will also provide you energy to manage or organise your house. If you decide to declutter your space, meditation will calm your mind and body and reduce stress so that you can do these challenging tasks without pressure.

For some of you, the thought of sitting still for a period of time with nothing to concentrate on is very unappealing. I was in your boat a few years ago before I took the plunge into a more mindful life. You don't need to spend hours sitting on your own in a room with your thoughts to receive the benefits of meditation. Why not start by building just 5 minutes into your daily routine? I'm sure you will be surprised at how much calmer your feel after a few weeks.

Practice Gratitude

This is an incredibly amazing strategy to keep you happy, but most of us don't practice gratitude daily. Acknowledging the blessings you have in your life will offer satisfaction. You will feel you have enough to live a good life and feel fulfilled. By practising gratitude, you can change how you perceive shopping. When you feel happy with whatever you have, no marketing tactic or desire can force you to purchase unnecessary things.

There are multiple ways to practice gratitude. You can maintain a journal of things you are grateful for. Every night before bed, or first thing in the morning, think about three things you are grateful for and write them down. Show gratitude when others go out of their way to help you, and be thankful for all that you currently have.

Go Outside

Happiness can be maximised outside your house. Getting into the fresh air can improve happiness. Some studies indicate that spending just 15 minutes outside in pleasant weather, whether walking, sitting, or playing outside, can boost a positive mood, improve working memory, and broaden your thinking.

This is good news for busy individuals who want instant methods to feel happy. You can easily invest fifteen minutes of your lunch break or commute to get some fresh air. You can double its benefits by spending time around nature, going for a walk near the sea or in a forest.

Practice Smiling

This may seem bizarre, but smiling can help you feel happy. Smiling can make you feel better after a busy and stressful day. It becomes more effective when we smile by thinking about positive thoughts.

This will boost your mood, improve your attention, and helps you perform cognitive tasks.

Most importantly, smiling can improve your ability to think holistically. This can help you make informed decisions that impact different aspects of your life, including overconsumption behaviours and impulse buying. Of course, you can't smile throughout the day without any reason. But you can at least try to smile at every opportunity you get in your daily routine.

Chapter 2

WHY WE FIND IT HARD TO PART WITH OUR POSSESSIONS

Why do we Find it Hard to Part with Sentimental Clutter?

Many people think decluttering is easy, but it's not. One of the most common things that are difficult to declutter is sentimental items that evoke feelings and memories. Some of us come across old journals and photos, grandmother's jewellery, family heirlooms, baby clothes, or a dress we wore at a friend's wedding but haven't worn since.

While throwing out damaged clothes, empty bottles of shampoos, or broken things in your kitchen might be easy, disposing of your children's drawings, treasured memorable photos, or souvenirs from holidays is a different matter.

Sentimental items remind us of places, people, special times, and important events. They give us comfort and make us happy. We may also feel a sense of responsibility if these items, such as family heirlooms, are passed down through the generation. Decluttering these items is not easy.

So, why should we declutter sentimental items firsthand when they are so precious to us? Is it important to sort out, dispose of, recycle, or donate sentimental items? Our most treasured and loved possessions can have attachments and hold great meaning to us that can be way beyond their actual monetary value. So, why would anyone want to declutter them? There are several benefits of decluttering and keeping your house clean and organised, including freeing up your energy and time for the rest of your life.

If you have limited space, the obvious benefit of less clutter is more space. Also, you don't need great storage space if you have fewer items. And you can easily find things in your storage when needed. But when you have to declutter sentimental items, the advantages we get by decluttering spaces get overridden when dealing with the emotional aspects of letting go of items that symbolise memories, love, friendship, and relationships. Hence, our hearts rule our heads. However, if you collect things to the point that they take over your life and home, causing pain, anxiety, and stress due to being a memory of the past, they become sentimental clutter.

Research also indicates that trauma and genetics can make people more sentimental and emotional than others, which causes them to collect sentimental items. So, if you have collected items as a memory, it will only harm you. Start decluttering your sentimental items to make your life easier and simpler.

Find a Balance to Declutter Sentimental Items

When sorting out, arranging, and disposing of your sentimental clutter, the goal is not to throw everything away. It's totally fine to keep some items that are close to your heart. The right way is to find the balance between keeping sentimental things that have an emotional impact and throwing away clutter.

You may also agree that when we have so many sentimental items, they lose their speciality and typically get lost among the clutter. We start feeling overwhelmed, burdened, or stressed by our sentimental clutter, especially if it's in high quantity. And when we have too many items, we often can't manage, maintain, and enjoy them because they are in great quantity. But if you only keep a few truly meaningful and important things to you, they don't burden you and help you enjoy the memories. You can appreciate and value fewer items more easily.

Here are a few tips for decluttering some items and making the most out of sentimental keepsakes that you don't wish to get rid of.

- Keep Some Sentimental Items

As I discussed, you can keep some sentimental items in your space. The trick is to hold on to a few clothes, toys, or other things that actually mean something to you, and you are attached to them to the point that getting rid of them would make you unhappy. Remember that having fewer items does not reduce clutter but allows you to easily manage and use them.

Set limits for yourself that can give you strength and direction while decluttering sentimental items. Choosing limits can help you make intentional and informed decisions. For example, allocate one box to keep all your sentimental items in. Since you can only keep things that fit into the box, you will be more thoughtful about choosing which items to keep. You can also dedicate a particular cabinet, drawer, or small space for sentimental items. Or you can decide to choose only five important items from the clutter. Having limited space or a particular number helps you be more selective about what deserves to stay at your home. Decide an ideal limit for your house and life. Then, no matter how tempted you feel to keep everything, stick only to the number you have decided.

- Ask Yourself, Why Are You Saving Them?

When decluttering sentimental clutter, it's crucial to ask yourself why you are saving the item each time. What is the purpose of keeping it? Is it for your children when they get old? Is it because it's meaningful for you, or do you love it? Does it remind you of the best moments of your life? Every individual has different reasons for holding on to an item. But make sure to assess why you are actually saving it to make the decluttering process simpler. If you don't find a clear reason to keep an item, you may not value or need it as you might have thought.

Analysing whether you need to keep the item will reduce the painful feelings. You won't be overwhelmed when letting go of those items as much as you would have been previously. Let's take an example of a thing you are saving for your kids. Do you think they really want it? Would you love it if your parents handed it over to you? If your kids are older, ask them if they need it. In most cases, we save things for kids, but they don't need them. Be honest with yourself and listen to what your kids tell you.

•   Look for Ways to Repurpose or Use Sentimental Items

Find ways to repurpose or use them so that you can appreciate and enjoy them every day. For instance, rather than keeping them in a drawer, you can display them where you can see them. If it's jewellery, attire, or anything you can wear, use them more frequently.

If you can recycle and make something beautiful from it as a memory, then do that. You can make a quilt from baby clothes, an old gown, or any memorable clothes. Also, you can make jewellery from collected stones or beads.

Another great way to repurpose sentimental items is to use them as decor. Do you have something you can use as home decor? Then, display them on your walls, side tables, and in your living rooms. You can even frame sentimental items in a shadow box and hand them on your walls. They will add character to your space and allow you to appreciate and see them daily. Avoid buying generic decor items; adorn your house with things that are meaningful to you, items that share a story of your family and life. Test your creativity and think outside the box.

Find ways to use, repurpose, or display meaningful things so you can enjoy them in your daily life. This is also a sustainable way of decluttering that produces less waste and protects the environment.

• Take a Picture

I can understand how you will feel getting rid of the sentimental clutter. You may have a heavy heart and struggle to make decisions. But if you can't keep the sentimental items in your house, you can take pictures of them to treasure the memory of that item. Technology has made life easier for people. The pictures will not cover any space in your house and cause frustration, burden, and overwhelming feelings of having to deal with so much yet allow you to go back to the old times you never want to forget- whether it be your wedding day, childhood, or your teenage period.

Once you take pictures, let the items go. Often pictures of these items are enough to preserve the memories. You don't always need to keep everything that reminds you of good times, a person, or the worst times of your life.

• Be Gentle with Yourself

You need to be harsh while decluttering sentimental things. But make sure to be gentle with yourself and give yourself some grace. Decluttering sentimental items is a challenging task, both mentally and emotionally. You might be riding an emotional roller coaster most of the time, and some things will be hard to discard, even when you don't need them.

Be kind and humble with yourself. It's ok if you take much more time to declutter than you imagined. It's ok if decluttering your items is hard. So, take a break if you get tired, or give yourself more time if you want to take it slowly.

Furthermore, keep in mind that some things will still be hard to get rid of even after you practise the tricks and tips mentioned above. Maybe they are so special you could never get rid of them, or it's an item that reminds you of the loss that is still fresh from recovering.

Be mindful and wise while decluttering, but take care of yourself during the process by making the right decisions. Every effort and time you spend decluttering your space will give you more space, freedom, and time.

Why it's hard to get rid of "Just in Case" Clutter?

"Just in case" clutter is anything you don't love or use but want to keep for future use. When you come across something you don't need or use right now, consider whether it's "just in case" clutter. Ask yourself why you want to keep the item. If you find yourself saying: what if, just in case, or someday, it's a sign that it is "just-in-case clutter," and you should get rid of it.

For instance, you may be keeping a cupboard full of wine glasses "just in case" you host a friend's gathering in the future. Or you might be keeping several blankets you have not used in years, "just in case" all your family in another state plans to come to your home. Or you have collected oil paints so that you can use them in the future if you ever start painting again as you did in your teenage years.

Sometimes "just in case" objects can come from a practical or frugal perspective. You might be keeping an extra keyboard, as your current one is getting old and will soon stop operating. This way, you don't have to spend your money. It's also a sustainable approach because you can reduce overconsumption by getting the most out of what you already have.

To deal with it, you need to understand the theme that drives "just in case" clutter. Let's look into what leads you to such a situation. First, in words like "just in case," "someday," or "what if," you worry that something can happen in the future. Secondly, the worry is mostly common rooted in one of three common themes: procrastination, fear, or trying to be practical or frugal. These can be the reasons for your hoarding issues.

The problem is that when you don't get rid of things because of "just in case," it can add to the clutter in your house. It can also stop you from decluttering and enjoying the benefits of a clutter-free, clean house.

Not understanding the effects of "just in case" clutter will encourage you to buy more things from the market due to compulsive buying because you think you might need products in the future. Consuming things more than you need increases demand in the market, which motivates factories to produce more products and use more energy, water, and resources. Hence, this results in environmental effects like global warming.

Decluttering "just in case" items will help you change your mindset and shopping behaviours. This will prevent you from going to shops or checking online stores and buying whatever you find useful for the future. But before you start decluttering, you need to understand why you collect "just in case" items in the first place. What makes you think that you may need it in the future? And what makes you hold onto things for life? Here you will learn the three primary reasons for collecting items "just in case."

Fear that can Drive "Just in Case" Clutter

Sometimes you hold onto things because of the fear of not having enough or scarcity. Keeping things makes you feel secure and safe, knowing that you will always have something if you need it.

What if you need an item in the future, but you don't have it anymore? What if you regret throwing them away? You will have to spend money on things again in the future after you have thrown the current items away.

The problem with these questions is that they never allow you to live in a clean, organised house. So, don't let your fear come your way while decluttering.

Procrastination that Can Drive "Just in Case" Clutter

Another reason that leads to "just in case clutter" is procrastination. You might be holding on to things you believe you will need someday. Or sometimes, you don't want to decide whether to keep or get rid of them, so keeping them is easier. You may not be ready emotionally or mentally to make a decision. Maybe it feels like you are giving up on your future self, hoping that you will use it, or leaving your past self to use it. Most of the things you hoard due to procrastination are useless items, so if you can't find any practical reason to keep them, declutter them sustainably.

Practicality can Drive "Just in Case" Clutter

In some cases, people keep things to be practical or frugal. Simply, they want to save money and energy in the future. You don't want to get rid of things and then rebuy them after a couple of months or a year. So, you keep everything just in case you need them in the future.

We all know that spending your hard-earned money on things is not easy, and sometimes you may not even have a budget to purchase new things. However, this doesn't mean you should collect and keep everything to avoid problems in the future. This is because, in most cases, you will never need them, just like you have never used them in the last few years.

Practicality will lead to cluttering every corner of your house with magazines, lamps, books, or decor items. Or your cupboards filled with clothes or shoes or your kitchen cabinets so stuffed with crockery that items are constantly falling out. In order to prevent possible hardships in the future, it's not a good idea to make your present living situation difficult and frustrating.

If you are worried about what you will do in the future, here are a few tips to get the things you want without spending hefty money on them.

Purchase Second-Hand Items

Once you have decluttered your house and if you ever need new attire, shoes, tools, or equipment, you can look for second-hand items. Nowadays, purchasing pre-loved items is on trend. Many people who no longer need clothes, kitchen items, decor pieces, or machinery sell them on second-hand websites or apps. Not only do you get things at affordable prices, but also you will get good quality items. There are also many groups and pages on social media sites where people are offering pre-loved items.

Also, you can look for platforms that offer second-hand things at lower prices. Just make sure to check their reviews before you make any decisions. You can also buy items from your neighbours, friends, and family if they are willing to help you.

The best part is that you can find just about anything- from smartphones, wedding dresses, kitchen cabinets, wall paints, toys, bed sheets, etc. Just ensure they are in good condition and the seller is trusted before you buy them.

Rent Items

Renting is another great option if you ever need things. There are sites and apps where you can rent clothes, shoes, handbags, or technology items. Besides that, many different brands also rent out their products. This is an affordable way to get an item that you only have limited use for, as you will be charged a much smaller amount than if you were to buy the item. Because you are loaning the items from trusted companies, you don't need to worry as much about quality as compared to if you were purchasing the item yourself.

Borrow Items

The simplest and best option is to borrow things from your neighbours, friends, or family. Of course, they should be willing to provide you with their stuff. This can save you money and energy to rent or purchase second-hand products. For instance, if you want a new dress for an up-and-coming wedding or party, you can ask your friends whether you can borrow one from them. They might give you multiple options you can choose from, making it easier for you.

Borrowing things is great if you want items for a limited time, such as a day or two. Most importantly, be mindful of what you ask to borrow. Obviously, people don't want to give things close to their heart or memory of someone, such as wedding dresses or rings, passed to generations. Make sure not to ask too much from someone. Once you borrow an item, use it carefully, keep it safe, and return it on the day you have promised.

Why not offer to reciprocate the favour and offer your clothes and items to friends and family? You will feel great knowing you are helping someone as well as continuing to limit the impact on the Earth.

Decluttering: How to Decide What to Keep or Toss?

Let's suppose three pairs of beautiful winter boots are lying in front of you on the floor. Each pair tempts you- your vintage riding boots, classic black booties, and expansive ankle boots. You know you need only one pair, so how can you choose one to keep?

Well, decluttering will never be easy, and you will struggle to decide what to keep and get rid of. You might be overwhelmed by your decisions and don't know how you can handle them. But remember that you are not alone. Many other women who have to organise, clean, and declutter their houses feel the same. While it will be hard for you to part with your belongings, choosing the right things to keep and the right things to get rid of is important.

Here are some guidelines to help you pick what to keep and what to toss away to make your decluttering process easier and more effective. Keep these things in mind while you are decluttering.

Do You Need This Item?

Does the object have a purpose? Do you use it often? Is the object useful? If it is a high-value item you use often and costs you hefty money to replace it, keep it. Contrary, if the object is not useful or you can easily repurchase, then get rid of it.

Keep in mind there should not be a bundle of things you are planning to keep because of their potential usage or price tag. Think carefully about how many objects you can keep.

Do You Want It?

This question concerns whether the item is something you appreciate or adds value to your life to make space in your storage or life. Ask yourself whether the item will improve your life in any way. Would your life be any less if you removed this item from it? If you really want it, then keep it. Just keep in mind that you don't want everything. If you find yourself in this dilemma, the simplest thing you can do is to prioritise your pile and keep the most important things. The items you really need will obviously fall at the top of the list.

Will it Expire?

Expiration dates are not limited to foods, but they also apply to paperwork and documents. For instance, if you hoard bills, resumes from a decade ago, old invoices, or old health test results, you are only wasting space. Toss them immediately! An expiration date is also linked to the fact that the object has outlived its life. For instance, you might be holding on to your child's shoes, but they will never wear them since your child is an adult.

Are the Documents Nonessential or Essential?

There will be some documents that you should save without a doubt. This includes warranties, wills, financial papers, various licenses, tax returns for the past few years, at least seven years of completed returns, and insurance papers. Keep valuable documents in a safe area or fireproof lockable storage boxes to protect them. And get rid of all the other documents in your storage room that are not important. While you can simply discard them, looking for sustainable options is better.

Can you Rent or Borrow it?

Can you borrow or rent things that you are planning to keep later? Do they cost you a lot of money to rent them? Are they difficult to rent? Is it available for borrowing from any of your friends or family?

If you got yes in answers to these questions, you immediately need to get rid of them. Just make sure to sustainably declutter them by giving them to friends or family or recycling them.

Is It a Gift from a Loved One?

Many things we have in our houses are usually gifts. Since someone else gives it to us, we feel our responsibility is to keep them safe. However, just because someone bought you something doesn't mean you need to store them in your cupboard for a lifetime. You should accept it graciously and show gratitude towards the gift. Keep it if it's useful; if not, take a picture and donate it. Another sustainable way to declutter this item is to give it to your friend or a family member who can use it. This way, it will not produce waste and will help someone who truly needs it.

Do You Have Duplicates?

If you have two or more duplicates of a particular item, it's better to keep a single item. For instance, do you need two sandwich makers? Does one of them require repairing? Duplicate items cover great spaces in your house, especially if you have kept them in highly usable storage spots such as kitchen cabinets.

If you ever have to store duplicates for any reason, such as because they are expensive to purchase or will soon replace the current product you are using, keep them out of the way. Try to free up primary storage spaces so that you can store things that you use often.

Do You Feel Guilty About Getting Rid Of Them?

There are several things you have that you can't throw away only because you feel guilty. For instance, you purchased a new handbag with your entire month's salary a few months back. Now, you realise you don't like it and hardly use it. However, you would feel too guilty about decluttering it after working so hard to save for it in the first place. Or you simply decided to learn guitar and purchase tools and the instrument to learn it and then found it time-consuming and difficult. Note that there is no guilt in back-tracking your decisions or in removing things from your house that no longer support or serve you.

Do You Put an Item to Better Use?

There are some items that your gut tells you to keep, probably because you think you will put them to good use one day. Many items spent their entire life in cabinets or wardrobes when they should be used more frequently. If you are unable to find good use for them, it's time to lend them to family or friends or donate them. This includes items such as:

- Expensive kitchen appliances and gadgets such as stand mixers or break makers.
- Quality gardening tools and equipment.
- Costly, top-notch sporting equipment, camera equipment, kayaks, party tents, and skis.
- Special occasion clothes and unique formal dresses or suits.

Chapter 3

TIDY HOUSE, TIDY MIND

Benefits of Decluttering

C lutter is not just the items on the floor. It's anything that impacts your life and makes it hard to live. Untidy environments often lead to stress for most people. In a study, women who describe their houses with positive language have a lower cortisol level, a stress hormone, than women who describe their houses as unfinished or cluttered. Another research indicates that our environment can negatively or positively impact our ability to complete tasks and affects our mood and mental health. Experts also suggest that orderly environments are more associated with healthy choices, while messy and disorderly spaces promote fresh ideas and creativity. If you value creativity, you may need to allow yourself to get a little bit messy in some areas of your life.

However, for most people, decluttering can improve physical and mental health. If the physical space around you is scattered, your mental space will feel the same. You can reduce anxiety and distress by removing or controlling clutter in your house or your personal space. Eventually, this makes you much happier, more confident, and less depressed. Most importantly, clutter can cause frustration and a burden on your shoulder, impacting your productivity and ability to make decisions. You might even notice that when you come home and find your room unorganised or untidy, you feel stressed, and suddenly your mood worsens. This is because of the significant impact of clutter on your mind.

The clutter in your space can also cause accidents and injuries. For example, you might walk on a toy when the lights are off and hurt your feet. Or you might fall on the stack of magazines on the floor just to find space to walk through the room without removing things, leading to injuries. By decluttering, you can ensure to protect yourself and your family.

Not only can decluttering help you get rid of unnecessary items and offer you a tidy and clean house, but it also makes you feel good about yourself. When you declutter your space, you feel accomplished, which makes you proud that you have done a challenging task. Furthermore, if you choose sustainable decluttering methods, it boosts your mood and gives a sense of peace to you because you are trying to protect the Earth. Sustainable decluttering can go a long way, especially if you stop overconsuming and impulse buying behaviours afterwards.

Decluttering sustainably has unconditional benefits. By understanding them, you might decide to change your life. Let's learn some most impactful and life-changing benefits of decluttering.

Benefit#1: Your Physical Health Improves

A clutter-free environment positively impacts your physical health in multiple ways. Decluttering your spaces makes your house much easier to maintain and clean. A cleaner home leads to fewer bugs and germs, which saves you from getting ill due to viruses and bacteria. Decluttering can also reduce mould, dust, and mildew in your house. It can also prevent the risk of pests in your spaces. All these things can trigger allergies and asthma that can drastically impact your physical health and get severe.

Decluttering also makes regular tasks like cooking and cleaning achievable and less stressful, preventing you from putting a lot more energy and effort into doing little things. This way, your body doesn't get burnout and suffer from aches just because of not being able to complete small tasks.

Excellent physical health is not just about living without any health issues. It is about living with an energetic, pain-free, and fresh body.

This is what a clutter-free environment provides you. Your body doesn't feel overwhelmed and burdened, and you can also avoid injuries by stepping on to clutter, falling on the floor due to disorganised spaces, or stubbing your toe on furniture lying in the middle of the room.

Experts believe a clean home is the main factor affecting physical activity. The cleaner and tidier the home, the more likely participants are willing to indulge in exercise. Physical activities will reduce the risk of cardiovascular issues, prevent diabetes, reduce the risk of obesity, and offer other health benefits. And let's not forget that cleaning or organising your space can be a workout in itself. So, if you believe your physical health has greatly been compromised in the past few years, look around and see if you need to eliminate unwanted items.

Benefit#2: You will be Less Stressed

A clutter-free environment is a lot more relaxing to be in. We hold on to items or collect unnecessary things in our houses for several reasons- we get busy in our lives, and clutter will inevitably build up in our spaces. But we need to acknowledge that no matter how busy we are, we aren't doing any favours to ourselves by not decluttering our spaces. Not to mention, research indicates clutter can impact our mental health. It causes anxiety, makes people depressed, and increases the stress hormone cortisol level. It prevents you from relaxing in your own house.

Clutter can even trigger your coping strategies like overreacting. This means if a person has overeating habits due to stress, a cluttered environment can also lead to weight gain. The worst part is rectifying the clutter when feeling stressed is not easy. It can be challenging to overcome and deal with the things around you.

However, as you know that stress can be controlled by cleaning your cluttered spaces, it's best to try to push yourself a bit to start clearing out your room. Once you get halfway to decluttering, you will observe the change in your mood, a sense of accomplishment, and the beauty of your clean area. That encourages you to complete the task, declutter your space, and keeps you motivated to continue your decluttering journey.

You will feel good by choosing sustainable options for decluttering that don't produce waste and emit toxic gases and chemicals into the air. Not only will decluttering help manage your stress levels, but it'll also boost your happy hormones when you realise you are actively playing a part in protecting the environment.

Benefit#3: Your Productivity will Increase

Women working at home need to have as few distractions around them as possible to focus on work. The same is true for any other activity or task you do in the house, such as cooking, decorating, or completing chores. If other stuff comes into your sight line, you might feel tempted to shift your attention to it instead of what you are doing. As a result, your work suffers. I have learned in the past, a few years back, that if anyone wants to be productive in their house, they need to minimise distractions during work. And yes, the biggest distraction in any house is clutter.

You will eventually become less productive if your spaces are stacked with clutter. As a result, more and more companies are now choosing remote working systems. This has made it important for our houses to be tidy and properly organised to make our office work simpler, seamless, and achievable. As a result, you will be able to meet your deadlines, efficiently complete your tasks, and actually enjoy working.

Benefit#4: You can easily find Things

When you find things you don't love or use, getting them out of your way can help you find things you actually need more easily. Decluttering allows you to organise your spaces, keep them tidy and clean, and assign particular areas for everything. So, whenever you need anything, you will know where to find it and be able and go and grab it easily. Finding things easily will save you time and energy. The less cluttered your house, the easier it is to find things. This way, you will feel less stressed and frustrated.

Many people, in fact, avoid doing a particular activity if they are unsure of where an essential item is. While not being able to find things may look harmless, it can make you significantly anxious and stressed, leading to self-doubt and confidence issues.

Also, you might decide to purchase an item you cannot find, even if you know you have one at home. Over-consuming things will only impact the earth and increase the production of items in factories. And if you find the lost item while you have already purchased the new one, you might throw it away, generating waste. Again, you will be causing global warming issues. Hence, not finding things will also impact your life and the planet.

Lastly, not being able to find things cause you to rush and stress about it. If finding things in your house is difficult and takes up much of your time, you will start feeling more overwhelmed, which can even trigger depression and other mental health issues.

Benefit#5: You get Better Sleep

Are you living in an extremely cluttered house? Do you feel stressed every time you are at home? If yes, then you might not have had a good night's sleep for ages. Cluttered spaces cause stress and prevent you from getting a restful night's sleep. Your brain will mentally process the external stimuli of excessive things around you and the thought that decluttering is a job that you need to do, but you are avoiding it to do. Additionally, sleeping in an excessively cluttered room is totally opposite to restfulness. Your room may also make you feel exhausted and like you need to rest. Even if you sleep, you will start to stress as soon as you open your eyes in the morning.

So, keeping your bedroom as less stuffed and cluttered as possible is important. If you have more space, you can increase the items accordingly. Also, don't make your bedside table a permanent home for magazines and books. Keep your clothes in the wardrobe instead of throwing them on the bed or floor. Try to make your bedroom your sanctuary, and you will start to get better sleep at night.

Benefit#6: You are more likely to Invite Guests Over

You might have been planning to invite your friends and family over for ages but haven't gathered the strength to invite them into your cluttered house. You might think they will judge you and give unwelcome advice, and these thoughts prevent you from hosting a wonderful dinner at home. While it's true that inviting friends over is not a great idea when having a cluttered space, socialising is important for your mental health. We are social animals that grow and succeed by spending more time with the people we love. Meeting friends and family makes us feel loved and gives us the confidence to overcome any problem. Our loved ones are our support system encouraging us to create a beautiful life for ourselves. They help us to avoid hopelessness and live our lives to their fullest. Having people who truly love and care for you can prevent depression, anxiety, and other mental health issues. Hence, occasionally inviting guests to your house is critical for your growth and mental stability.

Cluttered homes lack feelings of warmth and being welcoming. Instead, they are distracting, overwhelming, and chaotic. Therefore, if you want your guests to feel good instead of overwhelmed when they step into your house, you need to reduce clutter or adopt a minimalist approach.

The less stuff you have in your home, the more space you have to accommodate guests. Also, the more your friends and family will love to spend time in your house. In fact, they might even suggest coming to your house again if they have a great time with you. Whether you are an extrovert or introvert, you need a few family members or friends who can help you in difficult times, and they will only be with you if you find opportunities to meet them, that include inviting them to your house. So, start thinking about decluttering before any important day comes up to meet your loved ones.

Benefit#7: You have a Sense of Pride

Tackling big tasks like organising and decluttering is more satisfying than you think. Ensuring a clutter-free house can lead to a sense of confidence, pride, and self. You will feel proud of yourself that you have completed a challenging task. You feel accomplished, boosting your confidence and making other things easier for you.

Decluttering also helps you with self-love. Self-love is something that gets shoved to the side in order to deal with the daily busy schedules of family and work life. Decluttering your house and allowing yourself to live in a clean, tidy, and organised home is a big expression of self-love. This way, you will be choosing to do positive things for yourself. Something positive that you will enjoy and benefit from daily.

Keeping your home free from clutter will demonstrate that changing and improving your life is possible. You demonstrate that you are capable and competent, an amazing way to boost your confidence and self-worth and help you feel proud of yourself.

If you doubt yourself, it might be because of your cluttered house. You might not be able to clean your house, resulting in low self-esteem. Note that this can greatly impact different areas of your life, such as your personal and professional life. You need to declutter your room to make your life easier, boost confidence, and live a happy and healthy life.

Benefit#8: You will Boost Your Energy

Untidy, unorganised, and cluttered spaces can drain all your energy for several reasons:

- There are always things to do.
- You will notice things out of place.

- There is always a reminder that you haven't cleaned your space, which makes you feel less positive about your house and yourself.
- You have to continuously make decisions about your things- and the more items you have, the more decisions you need to make.
- You need to put great energy into the clutter to clean, maintain, and tidy it.
- There is always trouble finding things.
- You always feel the challenge to get yourself in and out of a room.

Whether you feel mentally or physically tired- clutter can be the primary cause. Besides that, there is also a challenge to rejuvenate your lost energy in spaces with excessive stuff. You find it difficult to relax, which becomes a vicious cycle of feeling drained from clutter and not being able to rest and recharge your body.

Energy is the most critical aspect of the body. If it's not there, your entire life will get upside down. So, don't let clutter overpower you and drain your energy.

Benefit#9: You will be a Great Model for Your Kids

Whether you have young children or want to simply show your kids how to run a house, showing them the importance and benefits of decluttering first-hand will help them in the future. Making your house clutter-free is a great idea to show your children how to stay organised. With your decluttering habit, your family can live a healthy and happy life. Since they will learn decluttering tips from you, they will never go through mental health issues caused by cluttered spaces. The best part is that you can engrain the habit of decluttering in children by making them declutter their personal spaces every few months. You can also teach them to avoid overconsumption that prevents them from storing things in their room. Besides that, teach them sustainable ways of decluttering so that they also learn about the importance of protecting the environment and encourage them to consume less.

With these amazing habits, children will feel proud and much happier. Teach them the importance of decluttering and show them how things work. Your decluttering approach can pass to generations.

Encourage your partner to keep their office workspace, cupboards, and other spaces clean, cluttered-free, and organised. This will not only help them avoid stress and lower self-esteem but also gives you a helping hand because you don't need to worry about cleaning and tidying your partner's personal spaces.

When the entire family practices decluttering techniques and ways to prevent it, your house will become a clean, relaxing and inviting space.

Benefit#10: You can Protect Your Children

Clutter and junk can harbour dust, mould, and pathogens that greatly harm your family, especially young children. It might surprise you that most people with hoarding problems have physical health issues related to clutter, such as respiratory problems. The clutter in your house can prevent air circulation, allowing germs, bacteria, and mould to thrive.

While mould or pathogen grows in the hidden parts of clutter, they can spread harmful particles through the air to the entire space, impacting the air quality of your room. You and your kids can inhale these particles and get ill. They can continuously attack you all, preventing you and your kids from living a healthy life. If you want your children to avoid developing any health issues, then decluttering is an ideal option for you. Also, you need to keep things clean to prevent mould production.

Another way clutter can impact your children is through accidents. As we have already discussed, clutter can cause accidents, and your children might not be safe around several items in a room. Toddlers and young children can pull things on themselves and injure themselves. Of course, you want to protect your little one, and the best way to do that is to offer them a safe place where they can play without worrying about anything.

Benefit#11: You can Save Money

Well, buying less doesn't always mean spending less. It's more about quality over quantity. If you have a properly organised space, such as a wardrobe, you will feel less inclined to buy things. Wondering why? This is because you have defined a particular space in your house for a specific thing and organised it properly, so you don't need to add anything. When you organise your house, you will notice that you have everything you need to live your life. You even notice that you already have things that you were potentially planning to purchase. You will be shocked when you realise how much fewer shoes, jewellery, toys, cutlery, or cosmetics you need. Decluttering helps you understand that you don't need anything extra. You can understand the difference between your needs and wants and fight off your shopping urges.

So, yes, you will save a handful of money. And since you are looking for particular items in the shops, you don't overconsume things regularly, which is a sustainable approach to living.

Benefit#12: You can Reduce Anxiety

Anxiety is an upsetting and debilitating state of mind. Some people suffer from acute anxiety, while others deal with anxiety disorder. Whatever anxious feeling you are experiencing, taking control of your space by removing unwanted and unneeded things can help you alleviate your anxiety. This makes you feel you have control over your life when you're anxious and stressed about something.

Creating a clean, cluttered-free environment and organising your space can go a long way to eliminate anxiety from your life. When you declutter your space, you will get confidence that you can improve other areas of your life that are the primary reasons for your suffering. Also, once you have full control of your home, you will have plenty of energy and time to invest in other aspects of your life to improve them.

Benefit#13: You Can Amplify the Beauty of Your House

Believe it or not. Decluttering can improve the appearance of your house. It makes your space aesthetically pleasing, welcoming, and calm. By removing the clutter from every corner, you can change the entire look of your space. The best part is that you can improve the façade of your house without investing money in remodelling projects, a new coat of paint inside and outside, or bringing new stuff to your house. Once you declutter, clean, and organise a room, it will make it much more welcoming and radically change the space. If you decide to sell your house, it could help increase its value. Having an inviting home with lots of space will also increase the chances of receiving an offer from prospective buyers.

Chapter 4

WHERE TO START?

H ave you made up your mind to declutter your home sweet home? Are you ready to get rid of unnecessary items in your life? That's a good thing to hear. But from where should you start? What are the steps of decluttering?

Well, decluttering should not be difficult for anyone, especially for women with families to facilitate. Therefore, I have mentioned steps for making your house cluttered-free that are achievable and can be practised for any space in your home. So, let's begin!

Step#1: Goal Setting

Before you make your way to the cluttered space in your house, you need to set decluttering goals. There are several benefits of creating goals. What? Well, do any of the following scenarios sound familiar?

- You start decluttering in full swing. After a few hours, you lose motivation and give up on decluttering.
- You want to declutter your house but don't know where to start.
- While decluttering, it's hard to decide what you keep and what you should get rid of.
- You declutter your entire house, but clutter seems to get its way back into your space.
- If you set goals for decluttering, you don't have to deal with all these issues. Clear goals will give you direction and reason.

Here are some benefits of clarifying your reasons for removing cluttered from your house:

- Having a clear goal offers you a destination, and having a destination helps you plan for the journey.
- A goal will help you create reachable steps that are less challenging.
- You will stay motivated when you have a purpose for decluttering.

- Knowing what you want to accomplish gives you an idea of what to keep and toss.
- Knowing the goal will give you a reason to maintain a clutter-free house in the long run.

Setting a goal is truly a great way to make decluttering easier and simpler. How can you decide on a goal? Here are some tips for setting achievable goals to declutter your house sustainably.

Keep Your Goal Simple

If you want to declutter your house, stop overcomplicating things. You don't need to write a long list of goals with great details. You can simply keep them on your phone, post a note on your tablet or write them down in a notebook to remember. You don't need precise details and a bulleted list. Decluttering goals are more effective when you keep them simple.

If you are someone who has tried decluttering many times but failed because of having many goals to achieve, then start small. Prioritise only one simple goal to get started on your decluttering journey. For instance, only create a goal limited to your bedroom, and avoid decluttering your entire house.

Be Realistic

We all feel dejected and sad when we are unable to achieve our goals. This leads to frustration, and you feel like giving up. It is important to keep your expectations realistic, sensible, and practical. Think about your capacity and abilities when you are setting goals. Keep in mind that you have so many other things to do in your work and life, and you want to avoid burnout.

Also, think about your mental and physical health to set realistic goals over a realistic period. Your goals should suit your commitments and life to achieve them successfully. Decluttering should not be extra work for which you have to leave all the other tasks of your life. It should fit into your life; otherwise, it will be a source of stress and burden.

Think about Your Why

What is the aim of decluttering? What do you want to achieve with it? You need to know why you are doing it and what positivity and change it can bring to your life. What do you expect to change through getting rid of clutter? You might want a clean house to protect your children from germs, to easily find things, or to create a welcoming and relaxing space. If you don't know the reason, you are more likely to stop decluttering in the middle of your journey. You will lose your commitment and motivation to improve the façade of your house. So, find "why" to keep reminding yourself why you are decluttering in the first case.

Don't Expect Your Friends and Family to Share Your Goals

If you expect others to share your goals with you, you might be disappointed. Decluttering goals that include other people rarely produces results. Every individual has different priorities, and decluttering might not be a priority for them, which is totally ok. If cleaning clutter feels important to you, set a goal that revolves around you and prevents you from relying on others. Others will understand you and the importance of keeping spaces clean when they notice an improvement in their mood and mental health. From that point, they may start to support you.

What do You want to Change with Decluttering?

A decluttering goal is more than just the act of decluttering itself. It's more about the transition you desire to use in your life. You probably may not declutter only to get rid of things but in the hope of bringing a particular change in your and your family's lives.

What do you want the process to do for your house or family? Whether it is to create space to clean and manage the house easily, make it easier for children to play, prepare to move, improve mental health, or reduce the burden from your shoulders. Make it clear when writing your goals for whatever change you are looking for.

Setting a Period for Your Decluttering Goals

Decluttering sustainably can be quick if you have a proper plan to succeed. However, decluttering becomes a challenging, tedious, and long task when you have so much stuff to get rid of. Your confidence levels are low when you have no proper plan in place. Hence, you may take longer than you originally thought. Therefore, when setting the timescale of each step, you need to be realistic about how much time you can dedicate to decluttering without impacting other areas of your life.

Do you think that you can clean the entire house in a week? Or do you need a month for it? Do you need help with the process, or can you do it alone? Make sure to avoid overcommitting or overstretching yourself. You need to think about your abilities and capabilities as well as your other responsibilities to decide on a time frame.

Remember, it's better to accomplish more than you expected of yourself and feel good and satisfied than underachieve and feel bad about your progress. If you are doing it for the first time, it's obvious that you will need time to sort out things, decide what to get rid of and what to keep, and choose the right methods to declutter your space. So, don't burden yourself. If you try to push yourself, you will eventually get bored or overwhelmed with the process and leave decluttering halfway through, which is not ideal. Take as much time as you need to make your house look organised and clean, and make it a relaxing space for you and your family.

Think ABOUT How You Will Know You Have Achieved Your Goals

Like any professional or personal goal, decluttering goals need a clear and defined result. Since you know your expectations from decluttering, how will you know that you have achieved them?

Will you know when all the bedrooms are clear when your child's toys are no longer spread in the entire house, when you have organised your entire bookshelf, or when you will be able to find your desired t-shirt or dress in your wardrobe without getting stressed out? Knowing the accurate result that ensures you have accomplished your goal will help you to stop when it's achieved. It will give you a sense of accomplishment and motivate you to move to the next step of decluttering. This approach will also prevent you from getting overwhelmed by doing unconditional work without seeing the results.

Get a Clear Picture of A Clutter-Free Space in Your Mind

When setting your goal and thinking about the results and expectations, close your eyes and visualise your clutter-free home. Imagine how it will look and how it will feel. What do you picture yourself doing? What emotions do you feel when you see yourself in a decluttered house? What changes do you see when you visualise the process? Try to create a clear picture of your clutter-free space and yourself in the house in your mind. Be creative and make it super real to truly feel connected with your imagined situation. The better you can imagine what you want to achieve, the more you will be tempted to achieve your goals, and the more likely you will succeed in your journey towards a clutter-free environment. Just make sure to do it in a peaceful environment where you can easily concentrate and focus your thoughts only to imagine your future clutter-free house.

Another tip is to think of how much your family will benefit from a super organised and clean space. Don't do it in a rush! Take time to get a clear and precise picture of your aesthetically pleasing, germs and dust-free, fully sorted, spacious house.

Find a Method that Suits You

Sustainable decluttering goals reflect what result you want, but simplifying and decluttering require proper direction and planning for the journey as well as a chosen destination. Therefore, consider what path will help you achieve your goal. What sustainable methods and techniques do you need to choose? What type of method will be perfect for your timeline and amount of clutter?

You need to decide on a decluttering technique that you can easily practice and doesn't need much energy and effort to stay motivated.

Example of Decluttering Goals

Now you know how to choose a decluttering goal, what things to consider, what steps to take, and what techniques to use. I have discussed some examples of goals that people usually have. When decluttering my house years ago, I also set some goals to organise and simplify my house. These goals helped me step up my game quickly and master sustainable decluttering. Let's learn about some examples.

- Discard expired packaged or unpackaged food items in the pantry or fridge.

- Organise, clean, or donate some clothes from your wardrobe.

- Clear out cabinets, drawers, closets, etc., to make them spacious.

- Sort through your documents and throw away or recycle any paper you don't need.

- Clear off surfaces like cabinets, desks, dressers, corner tables, coffee tables, countertops, and others to make your room look organised so that you get space to breathe.

- Organise your house's storage space, like behind doors, storage room, under your bed, etc., with boxes.

- Clean your car and get rid of anything you haven't used in a few months, as you will probably never use it in the coming years.

- Sort your medicine cabinets and discard any expired medicines.

- Donate anything you haven't used or worn in a year.

- Donate extra or duplicate items to charity.

- Sort through and sell your old books online, or simply donate them.

- Sort and organise your jewellery collection- recycle or get rid of anything that is broken, rusted, or damaged. Donate anything you haven't used in a year, and store the rest carefully and properly.

- Clear out shoes from your house that don't fit your feet- donate or give them to your family or friends.

- Sort everything on your dresser and assign a space for everything.

Step#2: Tackle Things Based on the Available Time You Have

Life can be busy. You might want to declutter your space and start living with less, but you might struggle to find the time due to several personal and professional responsibilities. The best part is that you don't need to declutter your house in a big purging session. If you have time and it works for you, progressing in the decluttering process will be easy and simple. However, it doesn't mean you can't declutter your house if you don't have the time and energy to spend the entire weekend decluttering.

Finding the right time for decluttering is challenging for women, especially working mums. You might juggle family and work, but it doesn't seem like you have enough time in the day for anything else. Even if you have time, you might be left with little energy, and decluttering is the last thing you want to do. If this sounds familiar, you might be thinking about how to find time to declutter. Here are a few easy and simple tips to clear the clutter from your house in your available time. These are amazing ideas to declutter easily and fast. So let's dig into it.

Know How Much Time You Have Available

Instead of just sticking to the thought that you don't have time, think about what little time you have throughout the day. It can be just a few minutes early in the morning or before going to bed. Keep a pen and notebook handy, or save notes on your phone. It will help you write down every small project you can do throughout the day. Every time you feel that you might get time for a few minutes after an hour or two, write it down.

Get the Most Out of Your Spare Odd Minutes

We all think we don't have enough time to get things done. However, when you look hard enough, there are always some spare minutes in the day. You might spend this time lying on the bed for those extra few minutes in the morning while contemplating getting up. Or sitting down to watch one more episode of the latest drama on Netflix, as the previous episode ended so dramatically, and you couldn't possibly wait until tomorrow to watch it. These are all snippets of time you can use to complete a decluttering project.

For instance, you can declutter one or more drawers when you have put a cake in the oven and are waiting for it to bake. Or you can organise the kitchen island while waiting for the kettle to boil. You can organise your wardrobe or dressing table if you have time between cooking dinner. Hence, you can do little tasks in the short time you get throughout the day for decluttering. While it's true that you can complete a few tasks in a day to achieve your goal, this approach is less overwhelming and stressful. In fact, this method makes decluttering more convenient and approachable for women with hundreds of responsibilities.

Choose Small or Easy Projects

If you have less available time, pick an easy place to start or look for simple projects you can complete in the required time. Just make sure that whatever task you choose gets finished in the time you have decided. This way, you will feel proud of your efforts and get your desired results. You will also feel motivated to move further with the decluttering process to accomplish your goal.

Small or simple projects can be anything. Suppose your goal is to declutter your bedroom so that you don't feel stressed whenever you open your eyes in a cluttered space and to make it more aesthetically pleasing. You don't need to clean the entire space in a day. You can clear out your drawers in the morning when you get ten minutes after breakfast, sort out your dressing table when you come back from the office, or clear out your side table while watching TV before bed.

This tip is helpful for busy women who don't have hours on end to declutter. But to get the most out of this technique, you must always look for opportunities to make your house clutter-free. Also, you need to avoid procrastination if you really want to change the appearance of your cluttered spaces. No matter how boring it looks and how tired you are, try to do one small clearing project a day. I am super organised and like to track my habits in my daily planner. When I started my decluttering journey, I added 'decluttering' to my habit tracker to ensure I did a little bit each day to keep the momentum going. So why not try something similar yourself?

Get Stuck? Move on!

If you begin decluttering tasks but get stuck for any reason, leave it for now and return to it later. Probably you are finding it difficult to get rid of sentimental items. Probably it might be taking longer than you calculated. Perhaps you don't have the right storage to set up to organise your things. Maybe an emergency comes up right in the middle of the task. It happens to many people. If you get stuck, don't get upset or tense about it. Think what the reason behind it and try to resolve the issues as soon as possible. You may find the solution today and start the project again the next day.

Practice 12-12-12 Rule

When you choose small and simple projects to declutter in the available time, you can fasten the process by practising the 12-12-12 rule. The rule is quite simple: locate 12 items to donate, 12 to keep, and 12 to throw away. This way, you can sort out most of the clutter in your spaces, like wardrobes, cabinets, and tables.

You can declutter the remaining things with other methods I will discuss, or simply declutter them how you like. The best part about the 12-12-12 rule is that it works for bigger spaces which are the most challenging to declutter. This method will sort out 36 items in the space all in one go. Don't wait! Start practising this technique today.

Try Out The 5 Second Rule

If you choose a bigger project to get rid of unwanted things, try this rule. However, make sure you have a big heart to practice this technique, as there will be no "if" or "might" in it. This 5-second rule can turn an extremely cluttered area into a simple and organised space in a short period of time. In this case, you need to pick an item and think about when you last used it. If you don't remember it in the first 5 seconds, get rid of it. The five-second rule will help you donate items you might have never used or not used in a few months.

Of course, you can make exceptions for sentimental items, but you should still declutter them to some extent. The five-second rule also helps you create a sustainable lifestyle and house that is easy to maintain. Even when you finish decluttering your entire house, you can practice this rule throughout the day to avoid collecting clutter in the first place.

Divide Massive Decluttering Projects into Small Tasks

Most of us avoid decluttering because we can't handle bigger projects that need time, effort, and energy, and we end up living in cluttered houses for our entire lives. Splitting larger projects into manageable chunks will help you make your space clutter-free. For instance, you can focus on cutlery one day, your worktops on another day, and crockery in cabinets afterwards. Breaking the project into smaller chunks doesn't mean you only have to do one daily task. It simply means you keep working towards your end goal while staying motivated. Once you break up the project, you can do one or more daily tasks depending on your available time.

Set a Timer

If you have small pockets of time throughout the day, you may not be able to complete even small tasks in one go. In this case, don't choose the tasks based on the project. Instead, pick the tasks based on the available time you have. Plan how much time you have and set a timer. Declutter whatever items you can until your timer goes off. Stop the task and get back to your other responsibilities. When you get time again later that day, follow the same steps and set another timer.

Choose Methods to Declutter

Before you begin decluttering, you need to think about what you will do with the unwanted items while decluttering. This will save you time during the process as you will not be confused and waste time thinking about what to do with the unused items.

Set out boxes or areas to put the items, depending on what you will do with them afterwards. For example, a box for charity, your local recycling centre, or donating to friends and family. If you want to practice sustainability, stick to donating and recycling methods, and only throw away anything which cannot be recycled or reused. In a later chapter, I will be giving you guidance on what to do with all of your unwanted items to minimise the impact on the Earth.

Step#3: Find a Place for Everything in Your House

One of the primary reasons our houses look cluttered and untidy is that we don't keep things in their places. Whether it's due to living a busy life or just not having the habit of putting things away after you have used them, this can completely damage the façade of your house. Not to mention, you cannot find things when needed. Therefore, everything needs to have a home or a specific place in your house. If you practice the technique of putting things away after completing decluttering, there will never be a stack of clutter in each corner of your space.

Whether it's the kitchen, bedroom, living room, hallway, or storeroom, they all have cabinets, drawers, surfaces, or other areas to store and organise different types of things you use in that particular space. And if your rooms don't have designated spaces, now is the best time to create them. Many people struggle to find a place for everything while decluttering. You should know that a place for everything is the key to keeping your house organised. But sometimes it's not clear where to put different things.

Wondering how you can assign spaces for everything in your home? Here are a few tips that you can try to organise your home and simplify your life.

Make it Efficient

The point of organising after decluttering is that you can quickly find or return things to their place. By placing things where they make sense, you make them easy and effective to find and use. For instance, you can divide the kitchen into different zones based on the tasks you need to do in every area. Keep baking pans, spoons, and other baking things near the oven. Keep all the dishes near your dishwasher to easily unload them.

Sometimes you might not be able to find the most effective place. In this case, you need to look for the next best place for the particular items. For instance, you should keep the vacuum with other cleaning supplies in your house. But you might not have space to keep everything together. In this case, you can keep a vacuum in the coat cupboard, garage, or other areas and cleaning supplies under the sink or in the laundry area. Don't worry if it's taking longer to decide how to assign places for everything. You don't need to customise every room to make space for everything. You need to be thoughtful in choosing the best places for everything to keep your house organised, clutter-free, and tidy.

Choose "Catch All" Spaces

No matter how good you are at categorising and organising things, things will always stump you. There is not a clear category for many things in your house, but there are items that you need. You can't just throw them away. You may need a "catch-all" to store them, depending on the type of items.

For instance, you can create a junk drawer to store all your catch-all that carries all the random but important and useful things in your house. A practical "catch-all" for the living room is a drawer that carries extra remote controls, different devices, and wires or leads to connect the TV with other devices. Also, a "catch-all" for kids is a big or small toy basket or box for random toys that can't be categorised.

Make sure that your "catch-all" is not as big as your room. I suggest you use the basket, drawers, bins, or small cabinets as a catch-all in your house. Only put things in catch-all spaces after the decluttering process to ensure there aren't any items you do not need or use. You can create catch-all spaces in every room based on the items you have. This will help you stay organised and save you a great time in finding things when needed.

Rethink the Space You Are Already Using

This technique is for regular items, such as wallets, shoes, keys, bags, jewellery, etc. Pay attention to where you usually keep these things. Instead of adopting the habit of keeping those things in new places you have assigned, rework the space so it suits your needs. For instance, your partner may come home and empty his pocket in random places. This makes your room untidy and makes it harder for him to find these things later. Instead, keeping all these things in a single drawer is best. This way, your room will be cleaner, and it will be easier for him to find every item. You can also put a box or tray in the drawer where he can empty his pockets. This will help you keep the drawer organised and use it for multiple purposes.

Step#4: Follow an Order to Declutter Your House

Excited to get a clean and tidy house but don't know where to start? If your entire house is cluttered, you need to choose the right space to start. Not choosing the right room can spread the clutter into other spaces, making things more challenging for you. So, if you want to keep your other spaces clean, follow a simple and methodical process. Here are some suggested steps you could follow:

Declutter#1: Storage Rooms or Spaces

- Garage
- Cupboards
- Drawers
- Attic or Basement

When I say storage spaces or areas, I mean your junk drawers and overly-filled storage spaces. The best idea is to start with smaller parts of your house before you deal with the more challenging areas. This will also allow you to practice decluttering before you move upward. Additionally, since you are decluttering, more than 80 per cent of the things you will organise and sort will be smaller items.

Remember that your stash places are where you can find a great amount of stuff you forgot you had or used a long time ago. You will find lost books, clothes, appliances, or utensils that you can place with other similar items. This will look like when you are unloading your food shopping. You need to clear and create spaces for them in the fridge before you can put them on the shelves.

Begin decluttering with spaces you can easily complete. For example, start with your drawers, then move to your wardrobes, next go to the attic or basement, and lastly, you can get into the garage. Of course, you can adjust the order based on the situation. For instance, if it's winter, you can wait to clean the garage until summer to make it a more pleasant experience.

While decluttering, you can also label plastic storage bins or boxes so that you know where you have put the things and can easily find them in the future. Then, again, you can designate boxes for donation or recycling so that you don't have to sort out things again once you have finished the process.

Declutter#2: Shared Rooms

- LIVING ROOM
- HALLWAY
- DINING ROOM
- KITCHEN
- BATHROOMS

This decluttering step is for the rooms that you share with other people. Your guests can also visit these areas. You need to start decluttering these areas in the second stage of decluttering. But if you expect visitors anytime soon, these rooms are the ones they'll most likely come across, so you can clean them at the first stage. Obviously, you don't want them to see your living room which you can barely live in because of the clutter.

Start decluttering them with the help of techniques we have discussed, like the 12-12-12 challenge and the 5-minute rule. You should also divide the project into smaller tasks to stay motivated throughout the process by seeing results. Keep the 80-20 rule in mind that suggests we only use 20% of all our items 80% of the time. This will help you think about things you have not used in ages and can easily get rid of.

Remember, when you pick an item, think if you have used it in the last month. If not, you need to discard it immediately. Experts suggest if you have not used something in a month, you are more likely to never use it again. To avoid getting emotional while getting rid of sentimental items, it's best to quickly perform the process. Don't think twice about discarding, donating, or recycling any item. The less time you take to decide, the more chances you will make decisions with your mind rather than your heart.

Declutter#3: Private Spaces

- Bedroom
- Wardrobes
- Home office/ Workspace
- Man cave

Now that you have successfully decluttered public areas, the next step is to clean private spaces. This is the third stage of decluttering because you need more time to assess the items you will find in these places. Stuff like papers, documents, shoes, and clothes will require you to decide what items to keep and discard. We all know these areas can be quite chaotic, especially if you have not organised them in a while. Unlike your kitchen, where you can easily sort crockery, these spaces will have more things that need to be carefully organised and decluttered.

Note that decluttering these areas can be time-consuming. It's better to get rid of the stuff during holidays or weekends. If you want to do it on weekdays, start with one drawer or one cabinet per day and slowly move upward.

Declutter#4: Move to the Remaining Areas

After decluttering the above-mentioned rooms, you can proceed towards the remaining areas of your property. These include guest rooms, laundry rooms, utility rooms, gaming areas, or other small areas in your house.

So, now you know where you need to start, don't wait and jump into the first stage. Decluttering is not easy, especially for women with bigger families and houses. The more rooms you have in a house, the more time and effort you will need to put into the process. Also, the time and energy will depend on how long you have collected things without decluttering previously.

If you live with others, it is best to ask for help to declutter. Your house is not only your responsibility but your children and partner also need to play their part in cleaning and organising the space. So, share your idea of decluttering with them and encourage them to help you. Discuss the best techniques with them so they can do the tasks easily.

The least they can do is declutter their personal spaces and avoid adding more clutter to their house.

Another thing to keep in mind is that sustainably decluttering your houses is important. While you will be cleaning your house, keeping the environment clean is important. Make sure whatever techniques you choose to declutter your home don't cause any environmental effects. Apart from this, once you declutter your space, minimize consumption so that you don't collect clutter again or cause a negative impact on the mother planet.

Tips and Tricks to Keep the Right Amount of Items

Consider the Space

As discussed above, everything in your house requires space, and you must keep everything in its place to make it look organised and neat. If you think you cannot keep all your items in that place, you need to declutter them even further to fit into your space. For instance, if you have assigned a drawer to put all your cutlery, ensure that all your spoons, knives, folks, and other things can easily be organised. However, if your knives don't all fit in the drawer, you may need to reduce the number of knives you own. Similarly, if you designate a space in the wardrobe for t-shirts, all your t-shirts should be able to fit inside the designated space. If not, donate some of them until they fit into the space.

You need to take a minimalist approach when organising your space. The less you have, the better. This way, you will use all your items- no shoes, shirt, or other item will stay unused for years until it gets damaged or broken. Maintaining and organising the house will also become easier and will take less time and effort. You don't have to spend hours cleaning or maintaining your house every week.

This tip will help you keep the right amount of items and get rid of everything that doesn't have space in your house. Getting rid of most things might be painful for you, but it will truly change the environment of your house. You, your children, and your partner will enjoy spending time in the house instead of feeling exhausted and overwhelmed by the things that surround you.

Remove Rubbish

If you have things sitting around that are not in the right condition to be used, you should not keep them, right? This tip is important to keep only the right items in your house. Having rubbish sitting around your house leads to a super cluttered environment. Throwing out all the rubbish in your house will create a massive visual impact on your house.

The rule of thumb for decluttering rubbish is that you need to discard any item that is:

• Ruined
• Broken

- Normal rubbish items: lists, old wrappers, etc
- No longer usable
- Non-functional

I understand that you might have kept these things in memory of something. They could even belong to your children and partner. However, throwing these items away can significantly empty your room, especially if you have stored a lot of them.

Make a box and gather all the trash items in it to see how many useless things you have kept all these years. If your kids and partner declutter their personal spaces, then ask them to do the same. Getting rid of rubbish leaves the right amount of things behind so you can further declutter to keep essentials. Just make sure when cleaning rubbish, don't throw them in the garbage, especially if it's plastic. Look for ways to recycle or donate them if possible. You can also try composting and enhance the beauty of your garden. You can also reach out to different companies who make products from waste if there are any near your location. Look for as many techniques as possible to sustainably declutter your house.

Only Keep What You Use Regularly

I bet there might be many items in your house that you have never used. You might have just kept them to use "One Day", but the day has never come in the past 2, 5, or 10 years. And the chances are that the day will never come in the future. If you have items you think you will use eventually but haven't used yet, you should remove them from your house. These can be clothes, shoes, furniture, jewellery, toys, cutlery, pans and pots, gadgets, equipment, instruments, and more. Adopt the rule of decluttering that if you don't use anything regularly, get rid of them. Only make space for items that you regularly use for different purposes.

By doing this, you will see that there are only a few things you actually use, and all the other items are useless. Most of the things you will get rid of will be items you have collected "just in case." So, don't think twice about decluttering these things from your house.

Think, Would You Buy It Now?

Another great way to reduce the number of items in your house is to consider purchasing them today if you have to. As humans, it's in our nature to change over time. Our preferences and tastes change as we get older.

Consider whether you have items you would never purchase today, no matter how cheap—remembering some? Get rid of these things. I am guessing that you will not have any sentimental attachment to them. And when you don't care much about them, you will probably never use them. They will only occupy your wardrobe, cabinets, drawers, or store room.

So, make it a rule for decluttering. If you don't buy it today, find a new home for these things. You can donate them to someone else who needs it.

There might be a few things that can stop you from decluttering. For instance, the item is expensive, a gift, or something you're emotionally attached to. Whatever the reason is holding you back, have a big heart and give them to people who will get the best use of them. Not doing so will only worsen things for you, as you will have more clutter to clear at your place.

Start Decluttering from Today

I know the idea of decluttering might be stressing you out. But once you begin to declutter and notice the great difference, you will get the motivation to continue doing hard work. All you need to do is take the first step and start clearing your house. Cleaning and organising your house is so captivating and encouraging that you will focus on the task and no longer feel anxious about it.

If you are still struggling to get the motivation to start decluttering your space, think about its benefits. When you have only the right amount of things in every corner of your house, you will no longer feel frustrated to find particular things. Your house will stay clean, and even maintaining it will become easier. If your guests suddenly knock on your door, you will not feel ashamed of the cluttered and messy environment.

Most importantly, you will become free of stress and tension and will feel more relaxed and at ease. You will no longer feel overwhelmed and frustrated when you enter your house. In fact, you will feel more than happy to live in a clean and tidy environment. It will provide mental and physical benefits that will improve your life. Aren't these benefits enough to get motivated to declutter your house? Don't wait; start taking small steps to clean your house today.

Harriet Webb

Chapter 5

STAYING MOTIVATED

Why Don't You Feel Motivated to Declutter?

Mostly, a lack of motivation is due to a lack of confidence. You might not feel like decluttering because you are worried you will not be able to perform the task efficiently. And, of course, the idea of being overwhelmed and stressed is not appealing to anyone. Therefore, you might procrastinate and look for other things to do.

If this feels relatable, one thing that may help is learning more about why you find it hard to declutter. You are not just organising and cleaning- there is so much more. We all have relationships with our stuff, even if we rarely use them. The relation with things is often rooted in your unresolved grief, fears of scarcity, or identity beliefs.

Knowing why you feel hard to part with your items will help you cut off the ties in an empowering way. Think why you don't want to declutter. Do you feel you will lose things that are close to your heart? Do you believe it's a tiring task? Are you struggling because of your busy life? Do you believe that you will feel guilty after throwing things away?

Once you know your problem, you can easily make up your mind about why it's important to declutter your environment. It's just not about getting rid of things. It's more about creating an environment that is functional, easy to maintain, and spacious enough to allow you to breathe easily. If you want to live a healthy and happy life, decluttering your house is the simplest way.

How to Stay Motivated Throughout Decluttering Process?

No one has ever said to you that decluttering can be easier. Especially if every corner of your house has clutter, you can't expect to enjoy the process. Many people feel motivated before they begin the process. They started decluttering in full swing, and when they finally started, they quickly lost their motivation after seeing how much work they needed to do. Well, it's totally normal. If you feel the same, don't worry about it.

You must practice staying motivated until you completely declutter your house. If you lose hope, motivation, and confidence in the middle of the journey, your house might never get in a better condition. You may end up living in a cluttered space for life or even add to the clutter over the years. Therefore, keeping yourself motivated and clearing out clutter is crucial.

Here we have discussed ways to keep you motivated throughout the decluttering process.

Break a Project into Smaller Chunks

When you start decluttering, you need to divide your project into smaller chunks. For instance, if you need to declutter your bedroom, don't start decluttering every corner. It's best to split the project into several tasks or small chunks. You can clean the wardrobe out one day, declutter your dressing table the next day, and get rid of things under your bed the following day. Divide the project into as many chunks as you want to ensure you don't feel overwhelmed and burdened.

When you are dividing up the project, make sure to make smaller chunks based on the time you have. If you are busy on weekends, opt for tasks that you can easily do on weekdays or break the smaller tasks even further so you can easily do them in 5-10 minutes. Furthermore, you can do bigger tasks on weekends if you don't have other things to do.

Smaller chunks of tasks will help you gradually move towards your goal. It will help you perform decluttering while doing other chores and maintaining your responsibilities. When you divide your project into smaller chunks, you can find some tasks you can ask your partner or children to do for you. This will make the process fast, and when you see you have help, it will encourage you to stick to the process.

Plan for Just 10 Minutes

Feeling stressed? Don't you have the motivation to start decluttering from where you left off yesterday? Don't aim to change the look of the room today! Just plan to clean your space for 10 minutes, and come back to it again the next day.

Often the idea of decluttering makes a person feel overwhelmed. You don't know what to do, where to start or don't feel like doing. Instead, if you only focus on a small area or a corner, you might find the motivation and energy to complete it. The tip is to sustainably declutter whatever you can in this area in just 10 minutes. In fact, set a timer on your mobile for 10 minutes and start organising and cleaning your space. The best part about this tip is that, in some cases, you get started and aim for ten minutes, but the task keeps you so engaged that you continue to do it until it gets complete, even if your timer goes off. But there will be some instances where ten minutes will feel like centuries, and you will run away as soon as ten minutes is over. And that is fine too.

You need to practice this tip every time you are not motivated to kick-start decluttering or are simply ready to get rid of things but don't want to opt for sustainable options because it increases your work. Of course, you can't declutter without effort and need to sustainably clean your space to impact less on Earth. But you don't need to push yourself. If you do, you might regret starting the project in the first place. So, start small, slow down, and aim for ten minutes of decluttering.

There are several high-impact decluttering tasks you can start with. When you lack motivation, you need to start with something that shows the immediate effects of decluttering in the area. So, when you see results quickly, you will feel motivated and will likely continue the task. For instance, clean only the upper area of your bedside corner. This will greatly change the look of your space. In fact, you will feel good sleeping on a bed whose surroundings are clean. Or you can simply clean your dining table and see the difference in your living area straight away. This tip helps you start reaping the rewards of a clearer and more spacious home, motivating you to continue the process.

Make it Fun

Fun? Can cleaning your house be fun too? Just because you are decluttering your home doesn't mean it can't be fun. You can combine other entertaining activities with decluttering to enjoy your time digging into your cluttered storage room. Some things that I prefer to do are listen to an audiobook, podcast, or music to make the process more enjoyable. Pairing something enjoyable with a boring and tedious task will make the job fun and motivate you to complete it. In fact, you will look forward to the time you listen to the audiobook, which will be decluttering. Keep in mind that you can easily adopt new habits when you make them fun.

Another way of making decluttering fun is to make it a mum and children activity. Doing something with your family always feels good. You will always find ways to laugh when you are with your family. You will cherish the time you spend with your children. Also, you can show them old things and tell them the memories associated with them. Most importantly, decluttering with your child is the best way to teach them important lessons about clutter control. As you work together, you can teach them methods to declutter, what sustainable approach they can choose, and how they can prevent clutter in the future.

You can do it with your partner if you don't have children. Even experts suggest that couples who spend quality time together can strengthen their relationships. This is because it gives you a chance to talk and connect. If you both don't have the time to go on a walk or arrange a coffee date together, you can declutter your home together for ten minutes daily. This is a great way to improve communication, enjoy some time together, and cherish the memories you will encounter while decluttering. This approach will make the entire decluttering process more enjoyable for you.

Don't Get Demoralised

Lack of support from your family can significantly impact your confidence and lead to less motivation. Don't get demoralised because your children don't like how you clean the house or your partner can't understand what or why you are doing it. Or perhaps your family doesn't understand what you are trying to accomplish. I know it can be hurtful and painful, and it might deter you from decluttering your house. However, your family will soon start to see its impact on the home environment and start to appreciate the benefits.

Keep in mind that you are decluttering your house to provide a clean and safe place for your family to live. When you lose motivation because of your family, remember that the piles of old and unnecessary things in your house can lead to mould and mildew. They can become homes for viruses and germs spreading throughout your house. Clutter can also lead to poor air quality. Therefore, whether anyone supports you or not, it is crucial to stay motivated and get rid of the clutter for the sake of your and your family's health.

For the time being, avoid what your partner and children say. Just focus on your stuff and your personal spaces in your house.

Celebrate Your Wins

If you have cleaned an area successfully, no matter how little or how much, reward yourself with something nice. Dance around the room, have a biscuit with your cup of tea, plan a family film night in your new living room, or enjoy a glass of wine while relaxing in the clutter-free areas. What you choose doesn't matter as long as you feel happy and accomplished after a productive decluttering session. Planning a reward before you have started will keep you motivated throughout the accomplish what you have set out to achieve that day.

Another tip is to create incentives for all stages of clutter control. Declutter one room, and you will get something, organise another room and plan a reward, recycle stuff, or donate your belongings and get something else. Opt for sustainable options to produce little to no waste. It's down to what reward you choose, but we all love working hard when something great awaits us.

Celebrating your wins is crucial at every stage of your life. It helps you understand how far you have come and how courageous you are. Celebration releases the happy hormones or feel-good chemicals dopamine, oxytocin, and endorphins. Therefore, you feel enormously happy when you celebrate yourself, and this increases with the incentives and rewards you receive. The boost in happy hormones can keep you motivated during decluttering, ensuring you achieve a clutter-free house quickly.

Do the Before and After

Looking for more motivation? Another best way to keep you motivated throughout decluttering is to take before and after photos. Many times we don't realize how far we have come. We don't understand our progress. Once we start decluttering, we quickly forget what progress you have made. But if we realise the quality and quantity of work we have done, we might never stop putting in the effort. So, take a before photo of the space you want to declutter. And once you get to the end of the tasks, you can take an "after" picture. Look at both pictures side by side to really see the progress you have made and the achievement so far. It will make you feel powerful and motivated to move on to the next decluttering stage.

Set a Realistic Deadline

Many of us can't focus on the work until we have a deadline. We procrastinate until we get bored and abandon the task halfway through, leaving it uncompleted. But when we have a deadline, we try to put all the energy and effort into the process until we get our desired results. So, set a deadline like decluttering the living room in ten days. Also, invite guests on the tenth day so you don't have any chance of missing the deadline. Attend a car boot sale on the weekend, so you have to declutter your house to get items ready for the sale.

While you will be setting a deadline, you need to ensure it's realistic so that you can achieve it. Furthermore, a deadline will help you avoid procrastination and give you a goal which is the key to decluttering your house.

Think About the Future

We all worry about our future and plan to live a better life in the coming weeks, months, or years. Experts indicate that the more connected we are with our future, the more motivated we feel about working for it. So, yes, you need to think about your future while decluttering.

What do you want your life to be like in a year, five- or ten years? How do you want your house to look in the future? What things do you want to improve about your property in the next few months? Are you looking for mental stability? Do you want to live in a clean and organised place? What environment do you want to give to your child? What problems do you want to solve for your family?

When you think about the answers to all these questions, you will understand why decluttering is important for the future - yours and your family's too. You will see that clutter control can change your life, mental health, and way of living. It will give a clean and healthy environment for your children to grow up in. It makes your partner feel less stressed and overwhelmed when they come home. Decluttering can make you feel relaxed as you stop worrying about your untidy house. It also allows you to focus on much bigger things in your life, such as your business or family, instead of thinking about cleaning your space daily.

Knowing what decluttering brings to your future will change your perspective and how you look at decluttering. You will also get motivated to improve your life and your family. This way, no one can stop you from cleaning and organising your house.

Start Practicing Self-Compassion

We all know that decluttering can be hard on your soul. When we clean our cupboards and wardrobes, we encounter many things we might have never needed. You will probably regret spending money and feel bad for your poor decisions. We all want to avoid encountering these uncomfortable feelings. This is why our motivation level decreases when we think about decluttering specific areas. However, you can turn things around by regularly practising self-compassion. You need to remind yourself that everyone makes mistakes, and it's totally ok. We all are humans and also perfectly imperfect. No matter how much you want, you can't change the past. But you can learn to form your mistakes and move forward. So try to give yourself some space and start to declutter as an act of self-care.

Join a Group

When you surround yourself with like-minded people, you start to think and act fast. You feel motivated throughout the day and feel the energy in your body to get through it. Keep in mind that people around you greatly impact your decisions. If your friends, family, or peers don't prefer to declutter their houses, think about choosing sustainable options, or simply throw things away when they need clean spaces, you probably do the same. Even if you know the right methods of decluttering and the importance of decluttering and sustainable cleaning, you might subconsciously follow them.

So, start surrounding yourself with people who take pride in their houses, avoid overconsumption, and practice sustainable living. But how can you do this? Well, if your friends and family are not into decluttering, you can join different groups and pages on social media platforms. Facebook itself has multiple decluttering groups you can join. These groups help you connect with people and discuss your problems. You can get advice and help from the experts. Since people in these groups have gone through the same problems and pain you do, you will also get the support that you are not alone. The best thing about these groups is that you can find many people who will just start decluttering as you do. You can talk to them and see whether they feel the same way you do. Feeling connected with others will give you the motivation to reach your goals.

Lastly, you can find success stories of people in these groups. They may also share before and after pictures and other details encouraging you to achieve your goals. Hence, different Facebook, Instagram, and Twitter pages can become your support in this hard time.

You Can Do Anything!

Whether it's decluttering, changing your job, starting a new business, or stepping into a new stage of life, it's important to believe that you can do anything. Keep in mind that there is only a fine line between your belief and goal. If you believe you can achieve everything, no one can stop you from reaching your goal.

It might take some time, energy, and unconditional efforts to achieve your goal, but in the end, you will definitely reach the place you wanted. In fact, expert suggests that those who believe they can do things that can improve their lives get to a point where they can easily achieve it. You just need to be consistent, never lose hope, stay motivated, and believe in yourself. You will eventually reach the point you always wanted. Believing in yourself is the first step to success.

When it comes to decluttering, this all might sound useless. You might be thinking that belief has nothing to do with decluttering. But that's not true! You will find the motivation, energy, and courage to jump into the challenging tasks when you believe you can make your house clutter-free. You will not think about "what if" and "how it can be possible." You don't lose hope when you don't see the results in a day or two. Also, you don't get easily anxious and stressed when someone tries to demotivate you and criticise you about your idea of decluttering.

When you believe in yourself, you don't need the support of others. You know you are on the right path, and whether anyone supports you or not, you can achieve it. Believing in your idea of decluttering will also help you get through every type of problem you encounter. It will give you the power to deal with the struggles and pain to get rid of things you have collected over the years. With this belief, you will be able to get less procrastinated and overwhelmed. You will always feel ready to clean your house until you turn your property into a beautiful home.

So, before you start decluttering and wondering how to get motivated, you need to start believing in yourself and your abilities.

Chapter 6

HOW TO DISPOSE
OF UNWANTED THINGS

Sustainable Ways to Dispose of Items

Consumer consumption has a great impact on the environment. According to the United Nations, more than 11.2 billion tonnes of solid waste are collected yearly. Reducing this solid waste disposal through methods like landfill or incineration is one of the best ways to protect the planet. But reducing waste is only possible when people take responsibility for the waste they produce. It's important that we consume fewer things so that factories need to produce less waste and we throw fewer things away.

Decluttering is also an important process that has the potential to reduce waste. You need to opt for ways that prevent your items from reaching landfills. In this case, you can start donating and recycling things. Practising sustainable ways in homes is critical to saving the environment. It will help to prevent waste from covering a large area of land. When you start recycling and reselling, it will help you save money and generate revenue.

Waste management can also improve sustainability. There will be less demand in the market for specific products. This will encourage companies to use less energy, water, and other sources to produce products. Waste can also lead to air and water pollution, and when you practice sustainable waste management methods, you can prevent pollution. The most important benefit of considering every step before you produce waste is that it makes us responsible human beings. We will ensure that we play our role in protecting our Earth. This will make us feel better and help us instil good morals in our kids.

For that, you must learn how to dispose of your items sustainably during decluttering. There are several ways that you can practice, but you must choose the methods based on the items you need to dispose of. Here I will discuss some of the most common items we usually get rid of and provide you with some ways to declutter them sustainably. So, read further to get some easy, simple, and approachable tips to dispose of items while decluttering.

Clothing

Okay, there's no doubt that you have many clothes in your house that you have not worn in the last few years. You may even have a few dresses, t-shirts, pants, skirts, or other clothes you have never worn because of their poor stitching or quality. And if you attach sentimental value to clothing, I can guarantee you have hoarded your child's childhood clothes. Besides that, you might have some clothes you wear occasionally or don't like at all. You need to get rid of these too. You only need to keep things that you wear regularly. Whether the clothes you are saving are expensive, branded, or remind you of a particular time in your life, you need to get rid of them. You need to avoid thinking about their sentimental value and the memories attached to them.

Are you wondering how you can dispose of clothing? What are the best ways that don't impact our environment? Here I have given you some easy, simple, and achievable tips to declutter your clothes. You can practice all the techniques or choose one that suits your needs.

• Resell

Selling clothes when decluttering is an ideal option that sustainably cleans your house and allows you to earn some extra cash. However, it's not that easy to sell your used clothes. You must opt for smart ways and uniquely sell your clothes to make the most money. There are several ways you can sell items from your wardrobe.

You can leverage the Facebook marketplace to list your clothes with details and wait for hundreds of comments and messages. This option is best as it helps you target a larger audience. On top of that, there are many Facebook groups for thrift items. Look for the ones created for your locality. You can use your social media accounts to upload statuses or post about your old clothes so your friends and family can purchase them.

You can also post your decluttered clothes on thrift stores and websites that sell old clothes. But of course, you might need to pay a percentage of sales to them or pay the fees to sign up as a seller. So, it's better to look for other free options if you want to make the most money from your old items.

When you resell, you need to be careful with the details. The sellers need to give appropriate information about the clothes to grab the attention of the buyers. First, it's best to make bundles of similar sizes, items, or styles, such as a set of jumpers or a set of jeans. This way, you don't need to sell each in a separate listing, which can get confusing.

One more thing – branded items sell pretty well! So, if you have any clothes with a known label, mention that in your listing. Also, while listing your clothes, always think about what you would search for when looking for something similar, and make it clear in the title and description of the item listing.

Give a description that includes the following:

- Type of item
- Condition- be honest. Some people won't mind if the side of a sleeve is slightly worn out if you are selling your clothing for a good price. Make sure you include any signs of wear and tear in your pictures.
- Size- write if it's small, large, or another size. This is important when people are filtering and searching for an item.
- If it is branded

Now that you know how to sell your clothes, let's move towards tips to sell your baby's clothes. Listing kids and baby clothes takes a great time and makes little money. So, keep in mind that you can't get a good resale price for kid's clothes. Here are the types of items that can get you incredible cash.

- Mass-market brands in top-notch condition offer good prices if sold in mini bundles.
- Popular mid to high-end clothing brands in perfect condition get you a good price.
- General brands in good condition work great if bundled together by age or sold in bulk.

If you have anything else in excellent condition, it's best to donate them. For clothes that are worn out or have holes, it's best to send them for recycling. Lastly, not all places work best for selling children's clothes. Do your own research to find the best sites to sell your particular items.

• Host a Clothing Swap Event

If you want to have fun after a week of decluttering and get rid of your unwanted clothes, then host a clothing swap party. Let's first discuss what a swap event is. A clothing swap party is a get-together that you can host in your house, garden, or any other place. Rather than throwing away or donating items you don't wear, a clothing swap event creates an opportunity to exchange your unwanted or unused stuff. You and your friends and family bring unwanted items to the party, and everyone can swap clothes and update their wardrobes.

Not only are clothing swap parties fun, but they also greatly benefit the planet. It's a great way to clean out your wardrobe with little to no waste. In fact, it encourages others to do the same. If everyone started to host clothes swap parties, we could successfully start to reduce textile waste. It might surprise you that around 1.2 million tonnes of textiles end up in landfill in the UK each year. Not to mention, the largest sources of textile waste are home textiles and clothes from consumers, which is around 85% of all the total waste.

Textile clothes are becoming one of the fastest-growing waste sources across the globe, let alone in the UK. Therefore, reducing consumption in the first place and opting for sustainable ways to discard your clothes is important.

So, why not set up a clothing swap party that will:

- Helps to save the environment.
- Allow people to get clothes without spending a lot of money.
- Help you save money.
- Allows you to declutter your wardrobe.

Are you convinced that a clothing swap party is worth the try? If yes, here are some tips to get you started in hosting one.

Look for a space that can easily accommodate at least ten people, such as a dining room or living area in someone's house. Community centres, churches, or libraries are some great places to host an outside swapping event.

Bring the right supplies, like hangers for clothes and fold-out tables for accessories and shoes. Don't place things on the floor. Your items need to be organised, and it's best to categorise them with size. Write the price and size description on paper and attach it to every piece with a pin. Create a dedicated fitting room area and install a full-size mirror in this space.

Let's get to the rules! Think about how many people you want to invite and how many items each person can bring. For a small party of around ten people, I suggest they bring ten items, including bags, jewellery, clothes, shoes, and accessories. Set and share guidelines on what people can and can't bring with them. You need to make sure that the items your family or friends are bringing to the event have the following:

- No stains
- No holes or rips on zippers or missing buttons
- That they are clean

It's time to invite your friends and family to your clothes swap party. Plan what you will do with the leftover clothes after the event. You can keep them for your next clothes swap party or simply donate them.

A clothes swap event is also a great way to raise money for a charity or event. People donate clothes to the party, and any money raised is donated to a particular charity or cause.

- Donate to Clothing Bank or Charity shop

You can donate clothing items to a charity shop or clothing bank. This is an ideal way to reduce waste production and support your local community. It's important that you only donate good quality items to a charity store or clothing bank, and anything of lesser quality should be recycled. Your old dress or jeans might become someone else's new favourite item.

You first need to identify clothing to donate. Look for good quality outfits in good condition from your decluttered bundle. Organise your outfits into piles and sort them again to rethink what items you need to donate. All your clothes should be clean and without stains. Wash and dry clean them before donating and avoid using fabric softener and fragrance-free laundry detergent.

- Upcycle them into useful things

We all know the three Rs- reduce, recycle, and reuse- but what about the "U" we never discuss? The U is as important as the Rs and stands for upcycling. Although you can upcycle many things, from old furniture to empty milk bottles, since we are discussing sustainable ways to dispose of clothes, I would like to turn your attention to your wardrobe. If we start to upcycle our clothes more than we throw them, we can keep them out of landfill, prolong their shelf life and help the environment.

If you are new to upcycling, it might sound intimidating to you. But don't fret! You don't need a sewing machine or need to invest much money. All you need is decluttered clothes and lots of creativity. Well, it's also fun and makes you so proud of yourself when you see the final results.

First, understand what upcycling is. It can be defined as "creatively reusing items." To be more precise, you will turn your trash into treasure.

So, what type of clothes can you upcycle?

You can upcycle any clothing as long as you are ready to test your creativity. In fact, clothing is the simplest thing to upcycle. You can turn your old jeans into tote bags, jean shorts, and household items like wall organisers. Some clothing items that you can easily upcycle include:

- Jackets
- Denim
- T-shirts
- Trousers
- Shirts
- Sweatshirts
- Socks
- Dresses

You can upcycle your clothes and turn them into the following things:

- Quilts
- Tote bags
- Scrunchies
- Rugs
- Scatter cushions
- Handbags
- Table runners
- Bunting
- Zip bags
- Picnic blankets
- Aprons
- Repurpose

You might be thinking that repurposing is similar to upcycling. Well, it's not. For upcycling, you need to be creative and put some effort into sticking, stitching, or cutting clothes to turn them into something new, useful, and appealing. But repurposing items don't always need effort. You can use the clothing piece directly for any purpose. For instance, the simplest way to revive clothes that don't fit you anymore is to alter them. You can donate them or give them to your friends or family. You can cut up unused outfits and make them into dishcloths and makeshift rags. Stuff your old clothes into pillows to make them softer and more comfy.

You can also cut a T-shirt into a halter neck top, cut your favourite jeans into shorts, or use a clothing piece to clean your shoes or bags. With repurposing, you can minimise the amount of discarded clothes sent to landfills. It can also help you decrease the production that uses raw or new materials, leading to pollution. The best part is that you can do these things with simple and easy methods.

- Compost Natural Clothes

You might be wondering what fabrics are truly compostable. Fabrics that have 100% natural fibres are decomposable. Natural fibres include silk, linen, pure cotton, hemp, cashmere, jute, and wool. But some semi-synthetic cellulosic fabrics like local, bamboo rayon, and rayon are biodegradable too. On the other hand, synthetic fibres like nylon and polyester are not easy to compost, so this should be avoided.

Composting natural clothes can help you truly impact the environment. It can help you make the most out of your unwanted clothes. You will also enjoy the process and observing how you can change clothes into compost to beautify your garden or vegetable beds.

- How Do You Compost Decluttered Clothing?

You need to start by reading the label. Check if the clothing is made entirely from organic fibres. Only garments made locally, naturally dyed, or by traditional artisans should be composted. You can also opt for the ones that are certified to be composted.

Ensure that the clothing is not stained with a garment from the do-not-compost category. This includes engine or cooking oils, paints, or other toxins. If you can remove them by washing them, then it's great. But if not, don't add them to your compost pile.

Eliminate all trims made of synthetic materials from clothes, such as zippers, labels, or buttons. Next, cut out any cuffs, collars, or hems made from non-biodegradable items. Cut each fabric into small pieces to rot or break down faster. Then place all the clothes into your compost bin.

One thing people tend not to consider when composting is that your bin needs to have a healthy balance of browns and greens. Compost "browns" consist of woody or dry plant materials like cardboard, paper, and dried leaves; in this case, it's your old clothing. They take longer to break down and are super rich in carbon. On the other hand, compost "greens" consist of wet or fresh waste like veggie peels and fruits, eggshells, and coffee grounds. They compost faster and are rich in nitrogen. When you have a balance of browns and greens, your bin will be composting most effectively and efficiently.

Making compost from your old clothes is a cost-effective way to make a blooming garden. It can also help your plants grow faster and healthier.

Toys

Toys are another common clutter in houses with children, especially if parents love to give toys to their children. While toys are important for children's growth and help to improve cognitive and learning abilities, too many toys can create plenty of clutter in your child's space.

When you see the toys filled in hundreds of baskets or stacked in every corner of their room, you might feel proud to give the best to your little one. But little do you know, the unorganised clutter might be causing a serious mental impact on your baby. Your children could feel stressed and uncomfortable while playing in a messy room. They may also get frustrated when they cannot find the things they want in the clutter.

Likewise, a messy kitchen makes it hard to cook and encourages you to rely on pre-packaged food. Clutter can also impact your child's homework. Experts suggest children have trouble concentrating in spaces with too many visual stimuli. There are many things to check out in the room, and therefore, less time to focus on the task.

Toy clutter in rooms can also result in sickness from unhygienic conditions, stress when others see the mess, and unable to learn tidiness from parents, which can impact their future. Clutter can be a powerful source of anxiety and stress for children. It can impact their mood and prevent them from participating in different activities. So, decluttering toys is important for children's mental and physical health.

While decluttering, it's best to opt for sustainable ways to dispose of unwanted things. This will also positively impact your children as they learn about more sustainable ways of living. I recommend shifting your mindset to purchasing more sustainably made toys using more natural materials than manmade plastics. This way, when you come to dispose of these toys when they are no longer used, you will be lowering your impact on the planet.

Below are some ideas on how to dispose of your unwanted toys in a more sustainable way.

- Donate

Donating functional toys for reuse should be your priority. You can donate them to childcare centres, shelters, and charity shops to allow children with limited toys to play with and enjoy their use. If you know people who might love getting used toys, take unwanted toys to them. Several non-profit organisations welcome donations of unwanted toys, as they will disperse them to children and families in need.

- Recycle

Recycling toys is not easy to do. Because a lot of them are made from plastic, it becomes challenging to recycle them. Many e-waste recycling initiatives take unwanted toys, break them down, and repurpose them to make new products. I recommend finding a company and their nearest drop-off point to take your unwanted toys (which cannot be donated). While these companies can help you recycle unwanted toys, they cannot repurpose every type of toy. Therefore, many toys produce great waste and often end up in landfills.

If you truly want to save the earth, it's crucial to stop buying toys specifically made from plastic. If you have the budget and find the opportunity, go for the ones that are either recyclable in the first place or are made from natural materials such as wood.

- Resell

You can sell toys in multiple ways, just like clothes. Use Facebook sale groups or sell toys at a car boot or tabletop sale. You can sell toys on several online platforms that allow sellers to list used items. Many toys like dolls, hot wheels, LEGO, and racing cars hold their value quite well. When listing these items, make sure you are clear about their condition. Show all signs of imperfections in your photos so that the buyer is aware of their quality.

Electrical Items

Every type of electrical item is made up of harmful chemicals such as beryllium, lead, brominates, flame retardants, and mercury. Therefore, improperly disposing of devices and gadgets increases the risk of dangerous chemicals contaminating the air, soil, and water.

When electrical waste gets into the landfills, it leaches into drinking and river water when the water passes through the ground. When contaminated water reaches natural groundwater, it has a higher toxic level, which can be greatly harmful if it enters bodies of drinking water. Therefore, reducing electronic waste is important when clearing out your house.

You need to opt for methods when disposing of electrical items that have a low impact on the environment. Here are some eco-friendly electronic items disposal routes that help to minimise waste pollution:

- Sell

You might have two coffeemakers or an outdated electronic oven you want to eliminate. These items might not be useful for you but can be a treasure for others, especially those who can't purchase new electronic systems. You can list these items on different platforms to sell them at affordable prices so people can purchase them and benefit with some extra cash.

You can list your microwave, sandwich maker, electronic grill, heater, and other electrical items on online marketplace platforms where a large audience can see your products and buy them at a good price. You can also try Facebook Marketplace, which doesn't require any charges.

There are a lot of websites that will buy your unwanted electrical items from you. Selling phones, tablets, laptops, and game consoles through these is a great way to get some money for your items. However, you potentially will not get as much as if you listed them on online marketplaces, but it is an easier and quicker process.

Whatever method you choose to sell your things, providing honest details about the product is crucial. If you don't do that, you might get banned by social media groups, websites, or any platform you choose to sell your electronic items.

- Donate

If you love to offer something to your community, donating electronic items to people will make you happy. Yes, more than shopping! In fact, research shows that helping others can boost the production of happy hormones. So, if you need a surge of dopamine levels, donate decluttered electronic machines, devices, and gadgets. Make sure they are in good condition, functional, and cannot cause any harm.

For instance, if you have bought an updated laptop for your home office, you can give your outdated computer to an NGO or student organisation. Or if you have electronic kitchen items like a blender you don't use anymore, you can give them to families who may need them. Before donating or selling your products, you need to ask yourself the following questions:

• Do the devices have any personal information?

• Is the electronic device in full working order?

• Do I still have all the cables and attachments for the device?

After that, you need to think about the precautions for donating electronics. Keep the following things in mind:

• Take out the batteries from the items before disposing of them.

• Delete all the files from your computer, devices, mobiles, etc.

• If possible, factory reset or wipe the device completely.

• Check the electronic items to see if they work before donating them.

Not every charity shop or organisation will take electronic devices, so it's best to check with them before taking your unwanted items to them.

• Leverage the Exchange Offers

Many retailers of electronic items have exchange policies that allow you to trade in your old devices and gadgets when you buy an updated version. They often offer you a discount on new products you are purchasing or will give you a cash sum towards the purchase.

Some electronic companies have established electronic drop-off initiates and drop-off points for items like tablets and cell phones after they are recycled. You can benefit from these opportunities to get rid of the items from your house.

Books

Whether you are passionate about reading fiction or nonfiction books or have enrolled in a program requiring a lot of material for studying, books can lead to clutter in many homes. Book collections have always been considered a good act and are often over-glamorised. However, having more things than you need causes unorganised clutter and mess in spaces. You might have a pile of books in every corner of your room that you no longer need. Or your shelf is just spilling out due to not having enough space.

It's great to have a reading habit or leverage books when it comes to studies. But it might not look great when it starts to produce clutter that impacts your mental health and can lead to mould and mildew production. Not to mention, clutter has a negative effect on reading habits. People who have book clutter reported that they read less and struggle to focus. So, if you have stacks of books that you haven't read in years, it could be a good time to start clearing them out. There are lots of ways you can dispose of your unwanted books. Read on to hear about my main suggestions:

- Donate to Second-hand Bookstores and Charity Shops

Used bookstores and charity shops are always looking for donations. They are also ready to take every type of book people offer. If you have used books that are still in good condition, you can donate them. Some charity shops specialise in taking used books, so it's best to donate to them if you have a lot of unused books. Where ever you choose to donate your unwanted items, it's always best to check with them first that they are taking the specific items that you are offering.

Donating is a great way for books to be used over and over again and for many people to enjoy them.

- Organise a Book Swap

Gather your friends, neighbours, and family, and trade! If you want to declutter old books, a book swap is ideal. Swapping books allows you to save money and helps you find new homes for old books you don't need. The book swap also lets you get your hands on some of the best books that can sometimes be costly and rare. So, if you want to have fun with books, go for this option.

- Donate to Charities, Schools, or Libraries

Check charities, schools, and libraries for donation boxes and book drives. Donating your books to people who need them desperately is the best. It's a noble cause, as you'll be helping someone learn and grow while they are saving money. This is not only a way to give back to the environment but also to society. If you have novels or old textbooks, donate them to book lovers or students who can get the most out of these books.

- Give them to Free Library

Free libraries are non-profit organisations allowing book lovers to find new books for free and share their favourite books. You simply need to take your books to these libraries and leave them for someone to take. On top of that, you can get one free book for yourself and bring it back to the library once you have read it. Unfortunately, not many free libraries are available in every town, so you will need to check if there is one in your local area. Search on the internet to find the closest one so you can visit it whenever you want.

- Use Stopping Method

If you are living a busy life or you have left with so many rooms to declutter, you can try stopping. Stopping means leaving your old items, like home decor, furniture, and even books, on your front door so people who need them can take them. This might not be popular, but you can introduce it in your town. This way, people can dispose of items without putting great effort into the process. If it's not common in your area, put a sign next to your belongings telling people they can take whatever they want.

Utensils, Knives, Pots, Pans, and Other Kitchen Essentials

The kitchen is the heart of any house. It is one of the most used spaces, especially if you love to cook. A kitchen is also where you enjoy spending time with your family and friends while cooking food for people. It's a place to laugh and joke around, share your cooking experiences, and have emotional conversations with your friends and family. Though this space is important, it can become a messy and cluttered area. You may find pots and pans falling out of the cabinets, spoons, knives, folks, and other cutlery filled to the top of the drawer. Your island might be entirely covered with unnecessary items, and you don't have space to prepare food. In this case, you might be thinking of decluttering your kitchen to make the space easier to use. To eliminate the clutter in your kitchen, you can practice the tips and tricks I have discussed above in the book. Wondering how will you dispose of decluttered kitchen items? Well, here are a few disposing options that you choose based on your needs.

- Ask Friends and Family

If you have bought a new oven, have lost the love for your oven and its functionality, or simply don't need it anymore, go and pitch to someone you might think will need it. You can give it to your neighbours, friends, and family. You can sell it to them or give it for free based on your needs. You could list it on an online marketplace or advertise it through social media your social media platforms to notify people who are close to you. Ensure that every item is fully functioning and not damaged before giving it to someone else.

- Donate to Charity

While many kitchen essentials can give you a handful of cash, giving kitchen utensils, crockery, equipment, and other items to charity organisations will give you peace of mind and make you feel happy that you have done something for the community. Just make sure that everything you give is spotless and is working appropriately.

Before you take your kitchen essentials to the organisation, contact them to learn whether they accept the things you want to donate to them. Some places have a collection service and can pick up large items from your house; otherwise, you can drop the items off at their centres.

- Recycle and Reuse

If no one wants your kitchen items, you can use one of the below-mentioned alternatives to protect the earth and keep them out of landfill.

- Contact the manufacturer to learn whether they run a recycling or reusing program.

- Ask whether they offer any discounts when you give them an old machine and purchase a new, energy-saving machine from them.

- Contact your local authorities who manage waste in the neighbourhood to learn what you can do with the items. Many will come and collect large kitchen items from your house and dispose of all the elements appropriately.

Makeup, Cosmetics, and Hair Accessories

All women love to embrace their features by using cosmetics and hair care products. The beauty industry is one of the biggest commercial industries, with a growing number of consumers due to the current social media climate we are living in. Beauty products are a great way to practice self-care and invest in yourself. While this is important, beauty and cosmetic products can lead to clutter in your bedroom, bathroom, or dressing space.

You may have bought too many foundations, polishes, lipsticks, eyeliners, etc. Some of them might not look good, but because they were expensive, you have kept them. You may have purchased new bottles without finishing the old ones. Or you could have been given new beauty products as a gift but are yet to take them out of their packaging. Sound familiar? I suggest that you declutter a lot of the items except for the ones that you use regularly. This way, you can make your space clutter-free, which will greatly impact your well-being. Your self-care routine will be greatly enhanced with a beautiful, clear space to care for yourself. Decluttering your makeup products will also help you throw expired items that can be dangerous for your skin.

But how will you dispose of all your hair, skincare, and makeup products? Here I have highlighted some of the simplest and easiest methods to dispose of these items. Let's dig in!

- Donate

Separate all the quality items that are not expired from your decluttered pile. Check whether they are clean and working. If yes, you can donate them to organisations working to help others.

Many women who can't afford to buy popular makeup brands or simply don't use makeup just because of their price tags can benefit from your items. But before taking them to the organisation, ask them whether they take makeup and hair products.

- Local Disposal Centre

Expired items which cannot be donated or given to somebody else often end up in a landfill. These cause chemical hazards when they are buried in the ground at the landfill sites. Many beauty brands are offering recycling services to help reduce their impact on the environment. Research what brands will take your old unwanted makeup items online and donate through them. They will often take all unwanted makeup, including items from other brands.

Why not encourage your friends and family to clear out their old or unwanted items at the same time? You can donate all of the unused items at the same time, doing your bit for the planet.

- Other Things

You can donate, recycle, or give several other things to friends or family. You can use the mentioned techniques for these things based on their quality, type of product, and method of composition. It's critical to think twice about disposing of any item to ensure you practice the right method and minimise waste disposal. You can take your time to research and make decisions on the best disposal routes for particular items.

Check with your local council on what they will collect from your home in their weekly curbside collections. Many will take away unwanted clothing, material, small electrical items, and batteries. You will need to separate the different items based on what they are, bag them, and leave them out with your recycling bin.

Check your local council website for what items they will collect, as this differs per region.

Chapter 7

MAINTAINING A CLUTTER-FREE ENVIRONMENT

Tips to Stay Clutter-Free

Y ou have done it! Finally, you have gone clutter-free. You have eliminated the heaps of clutter in every corner of your house and created a more organised and spacious environment. You might be really enjoying your house's soothing feel and beautiful ambience. Keep feeling proud of your efforts, and enjoy the new look of your house. But don't forget; clutter can return to your house anytime and any day.

Practising ways to keep your house clean, organised, and beautiful is important if you want to keep living in this wonderful environment. Think about how you can stop loads of items from creeping inside your house and taking over your life again. What items can produce clutter in your house? What are the simplest ways to keep your house clean?

Well, there are a few simple and easy things you can practice daily that save you from decluttering your house again in the near future. You and your partner and children should practice it together so that every space stays free from clutter.

Let's learn some tips and tricks to keep your house clutter-free for a long time.

Live within Your Means

We never plan to accumulate items in our house, which lead to clutter. It happens subconsciously, and then we realise our mistake after completely disorganising and cluttering up our rooms. Everything starts to build up again because you purchase new items without removing any from your home. You may not need these items, but you just feel they might be helpful in the future, or you just love how they work. You purchase things without thinking whether you have space in your house for them. As a result, you continue buying things without considering the size of your house.

So, to keep your rooms free from clutter, you need to think multiple times before purchasing anything. Stay away from compulsive shopping and impulsive buying. If you are planning to purchase something new, think if it can comfortably fit in your house without cluttering your cabinet, drawers, or other spaces. Additionally, think about whether you can do well without the item you want to purchase. Is it important to invest in the item? If you truly believe that the item is important and you have enough space to keep it in your house, only then purchase it. Once you have made a purchase, you need to find a space for it in your home, which could mean removing and disposing of another item. The one in one out rule is a great way to manage the amount of stuff you have in your house and ensure you don't slip back to your old ways of having too many possessions.

Declutter Your House Regularly

Many people who spend months to sustainably declutter their house stop cleaning, organising, and decluttering their house when the work is done. But this is what leads to the problem. Maintenance is the key. If you return to your habit of purchasing things without decluttering the old ones, you will again allow things to pile on coffee tables, bedside tables, kitchen islands, and dressing tables.

One of the keys to maintaining a clutter-free environment is to establish cleaning routines that help you keep your space organised and tidy. For instance, make a habit of putting things away as soon as you use them. Do a quick 10 minutes cleaning and organising session every night- teach it to your children too so they can practice the same technique. Sort your papers, emails, and bills daily to prevent them from piling on your living room table. Choose a specific time of the day to clean your kitchen. Make sure to sustainably dispose of any unnecessary items you notice in your house- use the same techniques discussed in the book. Schedule a routine for every task so that you don't forget. It will also help you avoid procrastination and the feeling of overwhelm. If you break the cleaning process down into manageable chunks and stick to a schedule, maintaining a clutter-free space will become easy.

Designate a Place for Everything

Whether the house is big or small, try to designate a specific area for everything. Do your best to organise items in their particular spaces. For instance, keep every type of cutlery in one drawer, pans in another, and pots in a cabinet. Never change the place of cutlery, pans, and pots, and adjust whatever types of pans, pots, and cutlery you have in that particular area. When every item in your house has a place, there will be no excuse for things lying around on top of surfaces or floors. This will also make cleaning and tidying up easy because you will know exactly where everything goes.

While designating spaces, make sure to be realistic and assign a place for things that belong to that room. For instance, create spaces for toys, children's clothes, and anything related to your children in their room. Keep your bedroom stuff in your room by assigning wardrobes and drawers for each type of thing. Also, encourage your partner and children to return items back to the places they belong to make it easy for the whole family to find things in the future. This will also help your house to remain organised for years to come.

Change Your Habits

If you want a big change in your life as well as your house, decluttering is not the only thing you need to do. It's important to adopt new habits to ensure you can maintain and sustain your new home environment. If you want to live in a clutter-free house with excellent air quality and no risk of germs and viruses in the corners of the house, you need to develop new habits.

Develop a habit of keeping things back in their spaces after using them, no matter how tired you feel. Ensure to recycle stuff that you are not using anymore. You need to stop your urge to buy new things and try to make the most out of the things you already have. Make sure to donate things that you don't use regularly.

Establish any habit that can help you keep your house clean, organised, and clutter-free. Adopting new habits might be challenging at first, especially if you need to clean and organise the house. But they will help you live a healthy and happy life. They will help you prevent the anxiety and frustration you experience when you enter your house.

Some of the habits that you can practice daily are:

- Placing daily-use things like books, clothes, and toys back in their designated areas.
- Reset a room before you leave it, so everything is in its right place when you next enter it.
- Establish a daily and weekly cleaning routine and encourage your family to get involved and help.

Keep in mind that some of your habits will depend on locations that act as clutter collection sites in your house. For instance, you may collect items like mail and schoolwork on the kitchen counter during the day, your one-bedroom may get a bit messier than others, or your living room gets a high volume of traffic every day. In these cases, you need to put extra energy and effort into cleaning and organising these particular places.

There are times throughout the year that may require you to put in more time and energy. For example:

- The need to store or sustainably dispose of excessive possessions after birthdays or holidays.
- The changing seasons may require removing clothes, shoes, and accessories from the house.

- Significant life changes such as new employment, a teenager moving out of the house, or childbirth will require you to adjust and refocus your space.

Not only do you need to change your habits, but your family members also need to support you by doing the same. Try to make them understand how important it is to keep your house clean, and encourage them to adopt your new habits as well.

Go Paper Free

Paper clutter is one of the more common clutters in our homes. You will only notice it when the attack of papers, mail, and documents will cover your living area, bedroom, and kitchen spaces. Paper clutter can easily build up if not managed properly. The best way to deal with the paper clutter is to reduce it in the first place and then put a system in place to help manage what is left. Going paperless is very easy. Assess the mail you get on a regular basis that is addressed directly to you. This could be bank statements, regular bills, charity donation letters, etc. Go to your online accounts for all the different things and select the 'go paperless' option. This will switch to you receiving email communications from the provider instead of through the post.

Next is to get a clear system in place for sorting the mail when it comes through the door. I find the following system the most effective:

- When you collect the mail from the letterbox, deal with it immediately.

- Put any junk mail into the recycling bin immediately.

- Set up two trays in an accessible place to file mail that needs actioning and mail that needs to be filed.

- Open all letters straight away and place them into either of the trays. Again any junk mail needs to be recycled immediately.

- Allocate time throughout your week to deal with anything in the 'action' tray, depending on the needed time.

- Once it has been dealt with, place it in the 'to file' tray.

- Once a week, file away all letters in the 'to file' tray.

- Now you have cleared everything ready for the start of the next week.

Change Your Mindset on Purchases

If you want to keep your house free from useless and unwanted items, you need to rethink your shopping strategies. Your purchasing habits are the primary culprit leading to your house clutter. Overconsumption is causing high demand for almost everything in the market. Consuming endlessly and mindlessly produces clutter in your house and causes a destructive impact on the earth.

When you overconsume, factories produce more products, using more resources like water and natural elements. This reduces the number of natural resources on Earth. On top of that, factories require a high amount of energy to produce products that again use our natural resources. Lastly, producing every item can generate harmful chemicals in the water and air. Hence, your consuming habits affect your house, pocket, and planet Earth.

If you love shopping and go insane when you see flesh sales and discounts in shops, you need to start working on your mindset. Developing a mindset that consuming things might not be a great approach for you can help you play your part in changing the world. You need to change your habits and perspective and need to practice mindful shopping to avoid collecting clutter.

I have already discussed in Chapter "1" that you need to ask yourself multiple times that you really need the item before purchasing it. Ask yourself whether you can function well without the products. Does it bring any value to your house or your life? How can it impact your space? Do you have enough room for the item? Do you already have an item that can do the same work as your purchased item? Can you use the item for the coming years? Is it environmentally friendly? Will you be able to recycle or replace it when needed?

Asking all these questions before investing your money in a product will help you truly understand whether you are purchasing it out of habit or need it. Also, to improve your buying habits, practice ways to keep yourself away from the idea of shopping. For instance, reduce the use of social media platforms so that you don't see appealing advertisements. Don't go to shops unless you really need something. Avoid taking any discounts, subscriptions, or anything that may encourage you to buy new things.

These techniques will also help you save money that you can invest in a retirement plan or a business or use to start a side hustle.

Practice One in One Out Rule

I know at some point, you desperately want to buy an item. You might need an updated coffee maker, new cutlery, a new dress for your friend's wedding, jewellery, or a toy for your child's birthday. In this case, you can practice the one-in, one-out rule. It's a superb way to prevent clutter from accumulating. One-in, one-out rule means that for every new item you introduce in your house, you need to get rid of an old item. This makes sense! When you dispose of an item, you immediately make space for the new one you bring into your house. This reduces any risk of pilling clutter in your house.

But when you choose an item to dispose of from your house, it should be the same type of thing you purchased or fall in the same category. For instance, if you have bought a new electronic grill, you need to get rid of your old one. But if you don't have a grill in your house, you need to get rid of any gadget, equipment, or machine to keep your new grill in that place. By practising this rule, you can avoid buying things you don't love or need and limit your belongings based on the storage in your house. Furthermore, you can follow this rule for items like books, clothes, gadgets, toys, or anything else that takes up space.

Make Donation a Common Practice

Many people who successfully keep their houses clutter-free regularly take out shoes, clothes, or unused items to donate often. While this technique is ideal, waiting for a specific occasion to make donations can also cause clutter in your house. This is because you might have several boxes filled with donation items in your storage or bedroom that you need to give to charity.

The best practice is to make a donation box that you can keep in your wardrobe, and whenever you spot something that you never use or wear, put them in the box. Once the box gets filled to the top, you need to take it to the charity organisation. Yes, don't wait for months to take your donation to the charity centres. This will only lead to clutter in your house.

Collecting donation items regularly will also prevent you from forgetting things you can donate. It keeps your house organised and clean and helps you get rid of things you don't use.

Choose Organisers Wisely

Here is a paradox: homeowners who love the idea of organising are typically drawn to every type of container, shelf, and box in the market that promises to get their house in order. But some of these organisers actually disorganise your house even more. In the beginning, they make everything look lovely and tidy. However, they soon become unorganised unless you reduce the number of items that you have.

Choosing the right wardrobes, drawers, cabinets, and workstation organisers is critical. They should be easy to use and super functional. Pick a type of organiser based on the space you need to organise. You can find different boxes and containers for spaces like Kitchen Island, drawers, and closets.

Also, learn how to use each organiser to get the most out of them. Ensure you use every inch of the organiser to keep everything in it. Remember that since you have invested in an organiser, it doesn't mean you now have the liberty to purchase whatever you want or keep everything you don't use instead of deposing them. Investing in containers, drawer boxes, and other organisers means keeping only a few things in your house to live in a clutter-free space.

Understand that Life is about Experiences, not Possessions

While the habit of shopping is ingrained in some of us, many people get tempted by the advertisements that make them believe that happy life is all about having trendy, modern, and latest things- an outdoor kitchen, a new car, and updated washing machine, high-end laptop, etc. However, this book may have helped you understand that it's not true. Happiness doesn't come from things- it's merely the experience you get through shopping. As soon as you purchase a thing, you will soon get back to the emotions you felt before you started thinking about shopping.

I know that the surge of dopamine levels is too high to believe this fact. But think of the last time you brought an item. Did you feel excited and happy when you brought it home? Or did you regret your purchase afterwards or simply didn't feel happy? The chances are that if you haven't regretted it, you at least don't feel the same level of joy that you felt while making the purchase. Realising this fact can truly change your life. Every time you visit an online store or step into a physical store, think about the truth behind why you want to purchase an item. It will remind you that the experience just tempts you and that you don't really need the thing you want to purchase. You will soon get out of the trap of constantly wanting to buy new things and will find yourself closing your web browser or physically leaving a shop once the awareness is there.

There are lots of things you can do to boost the production of happy hormones. And the best part is that the good mood you get from these activities lasts longer than shopping. Here are a few things you could do regularly to increase your levels of happy hormones:

- Hug your loved ones like a partner or child.
- Exercise daily for a few minutes, like cycling, push-ups, yoga, or swimming.
- Get a massage.
- Meditate.
- Spending time outdoors, either on your patio or in the park.
- Having a candlelit bath.

- Spend time with friends and family.
- Participate in things that you love, like cooking or crafting.
- Practising gratitude.
- Putting on your favourite music and dancing around the kitchen.

These experiences will make you feel good about yourself. They will make you happy, boost your self-esteem, encourage hope, reduce the risk of mental illnesses like anxiety and depression, and promote a healthy lifestyle.

Completely Reset Your House at the Start of Every Week

This practice can make a difference if you want to keep your house clutter-free. A deeper weekly reset can help you clean, declutter, organise, recycle and repurpose items weekly. Depending on what works best for your schedule, you can choose a particular day for the weekly reset. Choose a day you can entirely devote a couple of hours to cleaning the house without interruption.

The weekly reset means you need to get deeper with the cleaning. You need to check every corner of your house and dispose of items on the same day. It's your chance to consistently review what items you use in your house and whether there are more things you can live without.

Here are a few things that you could do on your weekly reset:

- Clean your kitchen cupboards, fridge, and freezer, and dispose of anything past its expiration date.
- Catch up on laundry.
- Gather the unused, broken, or extra items in your house and dispose of them.
- Declutter your drawers and cabinets.
- Clean all the surface areas in your house.
- Check your children's and your partner's spaces for clutter.

Once you put all you have learned into practice, the weekly reset will take merely an hour or two. You don't have to spend your entire day in the process. The weekly reset will get easier if you keep cleaning and organising your house throughout the week.

Put Your Clothes away after taking them off

Clothes can make a great mess in your house. In fact, you can see clothes everywhere in houses filled with clutter. If people only start to organise their clothes and put them in the right places, clutter can be greatly controlled. If your clothes are dirty, throw them in the laundry basket. If you are planning to wear them again after a few days and they are clean, fold them or hang them up in your wardrobe.

No matter how tired you are after coming home from the office or how busy you are looking after your children, you need to avoid tossing your clothes wherever you want. Avoid hanging your clothes on the back of a chair or on your bed and instead put them in their designated places, out of sight.

Remember, your bedroom is a sacred space; by putting your clothes away, you keep it that way. A clean and tidy bedroom will make you feel more relaxed, and you will reap the benefits of a better night's sleep.

Make Your Bed Every Morning

Making your bed each morning will reset it from the night before. It will make your bedroom a more welcoming and relaxing place when you come to bed the following evening.

I can also recommend opening your curtains and windows on a daily basis, even throughout winter, to allow fresh air inside your bedroom. Lowering the temperature of your bedroom is proven to aid in falling asleep, so the fresh air will help in many ways.

Forgive Yourself

We have gone through a lot of information, tips, and tricks on how to declutter sustainably, and you will not be able to put it all into action in a day or two. Some people take years to learn the best practices to declutter, control their consumption habits, and encourage their family members to also practice decluttering. Don't worry if you are struggling to get through the process and maintain a clutter-free environment. I struggled a lot initially, and with time, realistic goals, and persistence, I have managed to master the art. Remember that nobody is perfect, and nobody's house is perfect. In fact, the beautiful homes you see in magazines most likely have a team of professional stylists to make the house look aesthetically pleasing before photographing.

Of course, you don't have the help of experts, and you may not have much experience. You will need time to truly immerse yourself in the process, work out what works best for you, and make it a routine. Some people collect clutter again after successfully decluttering their house. This doesn't mean that they can never live in a clutter-free space. It just means they need a couple of attempts to fully learn this art.

So, it's ok if you fail to maintain a clean and organised house after decluttering. Try again and again until you accomplish your goal.

Chapter 8

HELPING OTHERS

When You Need to Help Others Declutter

When you learn the art of decluttering, it's time to help your friends and family to declutter their houses. Your loved ones might be struggling to declutter their spaces. They might be new to this and don't have an idea how to start and what to do.

Many experts argue that a person can do a better and quicker job if they declutter alone. This is true for many people. They want to make their own decisions and go at their own pace. It's also true that many people are not good clutter companions. They don't feel good when someone tries to make them throw something away that they want to keep. What you might think is clutter could be sentimental to someone else.

From my experience, I think it's best to have a companion by your side when you are a beginner. Obviously, a person with experience in decluttering would be great. A friend can help with the drudge work, morale, and decision-making. So, if your friend plans to declutter for any reason, you can support and guide them throughout the process. When you are with them, they will know what steps to choose, which room to do first, what things they can keep, and how to dispose of the items sustainably. You should, of course, not pressure them to make any decisions but advise them with empathy so they can understand better.

Helping a friend declutter becomes more important if they are going through a loss, experiencing a hard time, or dealing with health issues. It's hard to clear the clutter from every space without help in these situations. If your friends or family are facing issues and need to declutter, ask whether they need help. If they say yes, use your experience and knowledge to help them as much as possible. Since you have decluttered your own house, you have the expertise to help others. You can inspire others to maintain a clutter-free space and enjoy living a peaceful life.

I have discussed some situations where your friends and family might need help. When you declutter their house, keep in mind that they can be emotional about their possessions. You need to be humble and delicate with them to manage their clutter. Also, be patient and don't hurt their feelings. Read on to learn more!

Decluttering After Someone Dies

Clearing clutter after someone dies is one of the hardest things anyone needs to do. When clearing a house after a loved one's death, it's better to get support from others. So, if any of your family or friend loses their loved ones, stay by their side. Decide what you can do with their personal belongings, what to keep, and what to discard. These are some difficult decisions to make. The simplest way to start decluttering is by sorting items to throw away, keep, donate, and sell.

Decluttering after death is largely the same process as decluttering your own house. You need to sort the items by what you plan to donate, keep, sell, or throw away. The only difference will be that when it comes to keeping things of the person who died, you don't have to keep all their stuff. You should only keep a few things.

What to Keep

In the midst of grief, it can be hard for your friend or family to part with items that are the memory of their loved ones. Letting go of their stuff will feel like letting go of them. The process might be overwhelming and disheartening, but taking the plunge to make space and heal properly from the loss is very important. You can advise them to keep only important items that truly have value for them. Ask them what couple of items remind them of this person. What items can they truly keep in their house? Is this useful?

Make them understand that they can't keep lots of items in their house to weigh themselves down. By being very selective, they can reduce the burden on their shoulders. If they really want to keep all memorable items, they can take pictures of specific items and keep them safe for a lifetime. They can also repurpose some items by making throw pillows and quilts from them.

Tell them to avoid keeping items out of guilt or obligation. And remind them that it's ok if they decide to let go of things after some time. Make sure that they have patience and grace for themselves as they make decisions through their grief.

What to Throw Away

Get rid of damaged, broken, or items in bad shape. Throw away perishable goods unless the person cleaning the house can use them. Anything you can't donate, sell, or recycle should be thrown away.

What to Sell

High-end and expensive items can be sold through online platforms and marketplaces. For anything else, I recommend a car boot or tabletop sale. But keep in mind that the person cleaning the house should be in the right mindset to sell things. You need to prepare them for the sale so that they don't regret it afterwards.

What to Donate

What to do with someone's personal use items like clothes, shoes, or accessories? It's best to donate all of them. If there is any special attire that their family wants to keep, then they should feel free to do so. Make boxes for each type of item and write on them. Then, take all the boxes together to the closest charity organisation.

Decluttering When a Friend or Family is Moving Out

Is your friend or family member moving house? Do they need help with decluttering? You can help them benefit from your experiences. Decluttering before moving can save energy and time on both of their moves. Not to mention, it can also help them save money. The more things they have, the more money they need to move them. On top of that, if they attend a car boot sale, they can earn some extra cash.

Parting from belongings will not be easier for them. They may regret some of the decisions at every step. They could even try to avoid decluttering and plan to take everything with them. But you must continuously remind them why it's important to declutter. You need to show them the bright side of decluttering and keep them motivated. Remind them how great they will feel to eliminate excess stuff from their life, save money, and start fresh in their new house. Making them understand how to declutter can positively impact their mental health. You can also share your experiences to inspire and motivate them. Tell them how clutter control has changed your life. If they are doubting their decisions or simply confused, tell them how you felt while decluttering. Ensure to tell them that it was not easy for you either, but you did it to simplify your life. Remind them that you are here to support and guide them to achieve their goal.

Once they get ready, start preparing for decluttering:

- Set a date at least before a month they need to move and set aside a couple of days to complete the process.

- Make a list of items that they need to get rid of before they leave the house.

- Help them understand that "things that are expired will go on the list", "things that they have never used will go on the list", and "duplicate things will go on the list."

- Set a deadline so you and your loved one can do it under pressure and complete the task before the moving day.

After preparation, you can share the following tips to help your friend or family member:

- Work one room at a time.
- Mindfully decide what they need.
- Dispose of things with a big heart.
- Sort all the papers, books, and documents in the house.
- Segregate all the questionable items and then sort the things that you need to keep.
- Take out all the junk.

- Keep sentimental items that can easily fit into a box and take pictures of other items before disposing.

Decluttering to Help Older Adults

A study suggests that seniors living in clutter-free homes are 56% less likely to fall than those living in cluttered environments. Clutter control can also reduce stress and anxiety in older adults and give them peace of mind that they are safe. On the other hand, significant clutter in any space can lead to dust and allergens, causing various illnesses like asthma and dementia. Therefore, seniors need to keep their houses clean for their health. However, seniors don't have the energy to clean their houses alone. Since they have spent many years on earth, they are more likely to have collected many items at every corner of their house. It's best to support the seniors in your life so they can improve their life.

Remember that it will not be easy, especially if your loved one is sensitive. You will need to be extremely patient and empathetic with them. They might get distracted in the middle of the decluttering by seeing memorable items and treasures they have collected and refuse to go further with the process. In this case, you need to stay humble and remind them why they are doing it in the first place. Tell them the benefits of decluttering and how it can keep them safe from possible falls and illnesses. You need to ensure they feel good while decluttering instead of doing it out of pressure. Share your experience to inspire them to believe that decluttering is possible. It will be a painful process for them, especially when it comes to the point when you need to dispose of sentimental items. Respect their beliefs and opinions, and don't try to go against their decisions.

When you start decluttering, here are a few things to keep in mind to help make your house safe:

- Focus on furniture- it's best to remove furniture with the same colour as the wall, has sharp edges, or doesn't have easy-to-recognize handles.

- Clear the way- check the paths inside the house and try to clear any obstacles in these paths. Get rid of everything that an adult can bump into.

- Add storage space- add shelves and cupboards at an accessible height.

- Donate or sell items they don't use and are not planning to use in the future.

- Throw away all broken and damaged items.

- Make a list of heirlooms- ask the seniors to document their wishes for valuable items and heirlooms. Do they want to give to a relative or donate to a museum?

Decluttering a house for an older adult will take time. It's best to start with one room and work through each room methodically. When they see the difference, it will encourage them to keep going. From that point, cleaning, organising, and disposing of items in other parts of the house will become easier.

Tips to Help Others Declutter

I have already discussed some tips in each scenario to help others to declutter. But I want to mention some more tricks you can apply based on the situation. This will allow you to stay neutral and motivated throughout the decluttering process.

Use Gentle Language

Instead of saying, "The truth is you haven't used it in five years, I don't think you will use it in the future," say, "If you have other high-end cutlery, don't you think it's best to donate this to help others?" Use your words carefully and be humble with them. If they feel upset or humiliated, this could make them avoid taking the process any further or could impact your relationship with them. Changing how you deliver your message will completely change their perspective and help them understand your reasoning and logic.

Offer a Quiet, Helpful Presence

Often, people don't need your help at all. You don't need to do or say much. You can just be there, help them to think about the clutter, make an extra effort, and motivate them to make decisions instead of procrastinating. Give them advice when they ask you, and listen to their feelings and memories if they tell you. Allow them to feel safe around you. If they do it correctly by themselves, just give them a helping hand to move, remove, recycle, or clean things. Ask them how best you can help, and ensure you stick to the agreed role.

Point Out Their Reactions

Sometimes it is hard to know ourselves and how we feel about things. You can help guide people by pointing out their reactions to particular items. You can say something like, "You just said that you will never use that," "It doesn't seem like you really like that," or "I see your face light up when you hold that." Whether you believe it or not, this will clarify how they feel and think about particular items. Pointing out reactions will allow them to choose the right things to keep and throw. They will know what things they should donate or sell. Simply pointing out reactions can make the entire process easier and more joyful for both of you.

Make Sure You both have the Same Vision

For instance, if you are helping a friend who loves clothes and has many clothes in their closet, don't judge them and say anything. In fact, show your love for clothes to them. Tell them you will help them identify which clothes are best to keep and which may be worn through or could be donated. Ensure that you both have the same vision to avoid any conflict in the process.

Use Inspiration to Create Change

We all know that letting things go is one of the most challenging aspects of decluttering. Often, individuals with clutter know that they need to change, but still, they find it difficult. They procrastinate, get easily distracted from the task, and end up not throwing much away from their house. They sometimes feel pain and emptiness after getting rid of things, which prevents them from wanting to do it again. But when they know they are not alone in this, and others feel the same way, this might reduce stress.

Since you have good experience in decluttering, you can share your journey to inspire them. Tell them how difficult it was first you started it and how it gets easier with time. Tell them your steps, how much time you took, who helped you, why you decided to declutter, and how you maintain a clutter-free environment. This will give them the courage, energy, and motivation to get on the track of decluttering.

Understanding their Stuff is Important

If you want to truly help your friends or family, you need to understand that their things are important to them. You need to recognise why the particular thing is important to them. This will allow you to approach them with respect for their belonging, which builds trust. And the trust between you will help you agree to set boundaries and decide what to keep and throw.

Encourage them to see the Cost of Clutter

No one wants to lose time, energy, or money. Helping an individual find ways to save more time, money, and energy and eliminate frustration could be your gateway to help them deal with their clutter. You need to remind them how clutter can lead to health issues, possible falls, and poor mental health. If they are already facing any issues, you can point them out and encourage them to improve their life.

Allow them to Take their Time

I know it might be frustrating when you are helping someone, and they are taking ages to decide whether to throw or keep an item. It gets more stressful when they come up with a lot of reasons to convince you to keep the item they don't need or have never used. But remember that it's a natural behaviour. Anyone would do the same thing if they were in their position. If they are unsure whether to keep an item or are taking time to make a decision, create a space for a "maybe pile" for items to return to later. This keeps the process moving forwards. Avoid putting too many items into the "maybe pile". I recommend agreeing on a number of items that they can place in there before you start the decluttering process.

Contact their Family

The support of your family can make things easier and more approachable for the person. Having a family member on your side helps you deal with the emotional turmoil of parting away from memorable things. The family will constantly remind you that things are just solid materials. It is the relationships that are more precious and long-lasting. These reminders can help someone struggling to get rid of the clutter in their life.

Family can also offer support when a person declutters after the death of a close relative or friend. Parents, partners, children, or siblings can help with grief while staying focused.

Remember Your Experience

We often forget how we feel and how much we struggle when we see someone going through the same problem. Generally, we expect them to feel normal and avoid making a fuss about the experience. If you feel the same, it's important to remember your journey and hardships and to empathise with them.

Every time you feel yourself getting frustrated by the crying or stress of the other person, think about how you felt. Remind yourself of the challenges and pain you faced throughout the decluttering journey.

Help Your Relatives and Friends To Declutter

Decluttering someone else's house has different challenges than clearing clutter in your own house. Since you have learned all the tricks and tips to get rid of clutter, you might not struggle to deal with the things, but your relative or friend will surely give you a hard time. They may not understand why they should let go of most things or why disposing of sentimental items is doable. Based on their situation, they might also end up fighting with you or simply hurting you with their painful words, even when you are just trying to help them. In times of grief, people usually lose themself and struggle to stay positive. You need to try your best to ignore their negative behaviour and think about how much they love and support you when you need them most.

If you believe you can't help them to declutter or the process becomes too much, you can always hire an expert to help them. Sometimes it is easier for people to take advice from a neutral person rather than a friend or family member.

You can suggest hiring a professional organiser if:

- Your friend or family member is facing difficulty in making time to go through the process
- They are feeling overwhelmed
- They are indecisive and not making progress with your help
- You end up arguing over little things

- They take too long to clear the clutter of a single corner of a room

When you hire professionals, they will work with you to decide what to throw, keep, and identify where unwanted items go. In most cases, they will facilitate the sale, donation, or disposal of their client's belongings. They also work with you to determine the function of each space in your house and help set these spaces up so they can be easily maintained.

You can also assist your loved ones when they are working with professionals. Staying by their side and supporting them can make the process seamless. The best part is that the entire responsibility of handling your relative will not be only on you but also on the experts to help keep them calm and composed. The professional organisers are non-judgmental and respectful, ensuring understanding of the client's attachment to things. So, if you think your loved one will need more than one person to handle it, contact an experienced and qualified team in your local area.

Things to Consider Before Hiring a Professional

If a loved one dies, a senior you know needs help, or your relative is moving out; they may not have the time and mental capacity to try multiple expert teams to find the right one. Therefore, contacting an ideal expert on the first attempt is critical.

Here are some tips for looking for skilled, experienced, and trained people.

Vet a Professional Declutterer Experience

Look for the ones with the right credentials, experience, and good reviews. Research into how many years of experience they have to ensure they have been in the industry for a reasonable amount of time. You can ask to see photos of previous work they have completed or ask for referrals to learn more about their skills and experience.

Consider Goals, Timeline, and Budget

Before picking up the phone to contact a professional, discuss the goals, budget, and timeline with your friend or family member. These things will help you choose a suitable expert for you and can narrow down the search before reaching out to people.

Arrange a Consultation

Now that you have narrowed down some best options, arranging a consultation will be a good idea. Many professionals offer free consultations, while others charge small fees. Either way, you can't miss this step, especially if your friend or relative is sensitive about decluttering. The consultation will help you vet their style, personality, and work ethic. You will also know whether your loved one is comfortable having that person around their personal items or family belongings.

Discuss their Policies and Methods

Before hiring, you should know their policies and how they deal with the situation. Ask what techniques, tools, and equipment they use for decluttering. Make sure that they opt for sustainable decluttering methods to minimise the amount of waste from the house. Their policies and rules should rely on your loved ones' beliefs and opinions so that they feel comfortable during the decluttering process.

Ask about their Charges

Once you know your budget, finding a professional that can complete the task according to your expectations is critical. You need to ask for charges from every professional before hiring them. Professional Organisers can charge fees by different methods. Some will give you a complete quote to clean every space, others will take fees separately for every room, and many charge fees based on the time spent on your house. They may charge extra fees in addition to their standard price if your house is extra-cluttered. When you ask for the costs, they may schedule an appointment to evaluate the house's condition to give you an accurate quote. Some Professional Organisers have hidden fees that they could charge you at the end of the project. Make sure you discuss the total amount you will pay with the expert and get them to confirm upfront that there will be no extra charges.

Check their Location

If you want prompt services, you need to ensure your hired experts are near your location. Professionals in your local area should also know the rules and regulations for disposing of items in your area. They should know how to dispose of waste and what type of organisation will get ready to take items for recycling. These experts should also know of local charity organisations, so you can easily donate whatever you want.

CONCLUSION

"Decluttering Sustainably" is a book that reveals the importance of clutter clearing in our life. I have shared my experience with you to hopefully provide you with the skill and motivation you need to start your own journey. As a mum and wife, I understand how much people care about providing the best environment for their family. Therefore, I greatly emphasise to the readers to improve their lives and their loved ones by getting rid of excess items in the house to create a relaxing and welcoming space.

You now know that our love for shopping is one of the main causes of the clutter in our houses. You may get tempted by attractive advertisements, but the decision to purchase things is completely yours. Take the power back and control what you spend your money on. It's time to take responsibility for your decisions and rethink your behaviours and beliefs. Cultivate a positive mindset around owning fewer things, and get your dopamine hits elsewhere.

This book has also given you logical reasoning for why you find it hard to part from possessions, especially sentimental items. Start practising the methods to get rid of the clutter, whether they are sentimental items or other things. Use my tips to declutter the house effectively and efficiently. Ensure you keep minimal things in your house and dispose of unused items.

Keep in mind that I am not advocating decluttering just to improve the interior look of your house but because of its range of psychological and physical benefits. I have already discussed that sustainable decluttering can reduce stress, anxiety, and depression. It can help you reduce the risk of getting ill due to germs and viruses hidden in your spaces. Decluttering can boost your productivity and can improve your overall life.

Now that you have read the entire book, you already know what steps to take to clean the clutter from your house, from setting goals to creating a clear plan on how to clean the house. You have also learned my top tips for staying motivated throughout the process to ensure you reach your end goal. You have learned that the waste produced in residential areas is one of the primary causes of landfill. While we can't completely eliminate waste, we can at least try to play our part to keep your environment safe. Clearing out unused items can have a big impact on the planet, and that's why it is super important that you dispose of any unwanted items in a sustainable way. So, make sure you donate, recycle, repurpose, upscale, and resell all the items instead of throwing them into the bin.

When you have successfully completed the full process and are living in a beautiful, clean, and relaxing house, practice the tips I mentioned in this book to prevent the clutter from reappearing over time. Use as many tips as possible to ensure you don't accumulate more stuff in your house. Keep in mind the less thing that comes to your house, the less likely you will collect clutter. Hold the decluttering rules tightly and practice them regularly to keep your home clutter-free.

After reading this book, you hopefully know what it takes to make your house clutter-free. You know the struggle, the pain, and the anxious feelings that may come your way throughout the process. You can use your knowledge to guide others and help them through the same process. Help seniors who don't have the energy to improve their house, family, or friends who are moving out or someone who has recently lost their loved ones. Inspire others with your stories and make the most out of your knowledge.

Did you enjoy reading this book? Did it help you in any way? Was it inspiring enough? How has the book impacted your life? If you find this book useful, please leave a review and let us know your thoughts. Tell me the changes this book has helped you make and how it's improving your life. I love hearing people's stories and journeys and what they have accomplished along the way.

Printed in Great Britain
by Amazon

26098502R00099